How do I know when I'm ready to have kids?

CARLA SAVANNAH

Copyright © 2020 by Carla Savannah
Book design by Kristie Bradfield

www.kristiebradfield.com

This book is protected by copyright. No part of it may be reproduced, stored in a retrieval system, or transmitted in any form or by any means, electronic, mechanical, photocopying, recording, or otherwise, without the prior written permission of the author.

Contents

	Acknowledgements	v
Chapter 1	Awakening to a big issue within society	1
Chapter 2	My introduction to parenting	7
Chapter 3	Why do you want to have children?	16
Chapter 4	Going from bad parenting to conscious parenting	35
Chapter 5	Parenting styles	43
Chapter 6	Healing through my studies and experiences	52
Chapter 7	Can you prepare yourself for parenting?	58
Chapter 8	Postnatal Depression take two!	73

Chapter 9	Having children Step children	79
Chapter 10	The planned unexpected	91
Chapter 11	Parenting today	98
Chapter 12	My childhood	104
Chapter 13	The role of the Co-creator?	114
Chapter 14	Becoming your Authentic Self	139
Chapter 15	Men take the Contraceptive Pill	144
Chapter 16	Getting ready for kids	148
Chapter 17	P.S.	158

Acknowledgements

This book was inspired by my own experiences and mistakes within my parenting journey. Therefore, I feel it's only fair to dedicate the makings of this book to my children, but in particular my first born child, who rode the parenting rollercoaster with me through the challenging times as I was learning how to parent.

My eldest, I'll call her my Virgo, has turned out to be a thoughtful, generous, tolerant and kind young Woman. Sometimes I wonder whether I had anything to do with the conditioning of her personality at all. I really was lucky to have been blessed with a child of such a good nature. I love you, Baby Girl.

My other 2 girls got the better of me however I need to acknowledge that all my children were my teachers and if it wasn't for each of their individual personalities and roles they played in my life I wouldn't have become the Woman that I am today. My Virgo helped me to become a better Woman, My Scorpio helped me to become a better Mother and My Aries helped me to connect all the dots and grow into a better person as a whole within society. They were my teachers and in turn prepared me to become a teacher myself.

Of course I can't go past mentioning my step daughter, my Aquarian, who challenged me on a daily basis. Being a step mother to this Aquarian opened the door to lots of inner child work for me that needed to be done. I didn't realise just how many unresolved emotions I had not yet dealt with until she came into my life. She was so like me, she confronted me with my unhealed childhood self. My step-daughter helped me to open my heart not only to the hurting inner child within me but also taught me to accept and have compassion towards another human being that I have no biological connection to. When it comes to having a step child the natural instinct to protect them like you would naturally a family member 'isn't' there automatically, it's a behaviour that needs to be learnt, but it's not easy to learn. This instinct to nurture a step child is born out of the love that you have for your partner and the desire to protect something that is a part of them. When you love your partner enough every extension of them is a piece of them you naturally fall in love with also.

Thank you Miss Aquarian for coming into my life and teaching me how to extend my love reach.

I love and adore all of you girls!

CHAPTER ONE

Awakening to a big issue within society

Honestly, I'm not sure I remember what happened that led me to lose my temper with my three-year-old Virgo. I do remember however the impatience, anger and feeling of being disrespected coming over me and before I had time to calm down I slapped her across her face. Her eyes whirled up with tears, and blood began to trickle down her little nose. I had completely forgotten that due to the heat she was getting regular nose bleeds. All I thought was I couldn't have slapped her hard enough to cause a nose bleed, but obviously it did. Seeing the blood running down her little nose instantly sent me into a spiral of feeling guilt and shame. I put my hands to my face in disbelief thinking What am I doing?! Is this the kind of mother I've become? As I cleaned her up I began to weep "I'm so sorry!". The anguish of knowing that I just hurt my child simply for the need to maintain power was unbearable. I wish I could say this was the last of my regrets as a parent but sadly it wasn't.

I think most people will agree that parenting is the one role in their lives they don't want to feel like a failure at. If you are reading this book, then you are one of those rare people who actually cares about the type of parent you want to be. I've personally made lots of mistakes in my role as a parent. Some mistakes where because I didn't know any better at the time but most I have to take full responsibility for because I "should" have taken more initiative to have created changes sooner. I should have learnt more about parenting, experienced more time around children and done much more inner child work before I had children of my own. This immaturity did not only cost me my emotional wellbeing but it cost me the natural bonding process and connection that should have taken place within the first 5 years of my little

Virgo's daughter's life. That's a time I will now never get back.

I worry that as Women in society we take our right to have children very impulsively, without consideration for all lives that are involved in the decision. I see people choosing to have children selfishly to boost their self-esteem, satisfy ego needs or change their status in society. People are having kids to help themselves feel good based on what the child can do for them or give and fulfil within them. People often seek acknowledgement, validation and significance through their children. They create a false attachment to the child based on these ideals. When the child doesn't live up to the parent's ideals, attachment turns into "conditional" love. Meaning the parent only feels happy with the child if that child lives up to the expectations of the parent or does as the parent tells them to do. After all they are the only ones that know best…?

Children come through us but they don't belong to us. We are simply a channel by which they came through and they will eventually become a part of society separate from us. When we realise that a child is an individual from us and we start to see them becoming an independent self-expressive person, as parents, we start to feel as though the child no longer needs us. We see it as an attempt of breaking the attachment or connection to us. This simply is not true. Children merely are trying to become a unique expression of themselves within society. They are merely an extension of us. We actually give birth to our own expansion.

Our job is to learn how to keep them safe, give them a good foundation at the same time as giving them enough freedom to be an individual as a part of the bigger picture. This is probably the biggest challenge we face within our parenting journey. Knowing how much and when to let go.

In this book I will talk about how I overcame such hurdles especially with my teenagers. I will speak of my struggle with Postnatal Depression, raise basic challenges that parents may be faced with on and ways to overcome these challenges and become the parents they've always wanted to be. My hope is that I can save some people the heartache of my own story. I do this knowing that I'll come up against lots of judgement and criticism, but I ask that people look past my immaturity and ignorance at the time of my early parenting and absorb the wisdom and message behind my experiences and current knowledge.

Originally I thought of calling this book "License to become a parent" as I've always felt that there should be a compulsory program or course that people should take before having children. Maybe even making it a necessary course given in high school. Hopefully to reduce the amount of unwanted and unplanned pregnancies within society. Maybe even reduce the amount of teen pregnancy, but then the issue is not teenage pregnancy because I have met some incredibly mature teenagers who have made amazing young Mothers. Then I opted for the less harsh and less controversial title of "How do I know when I'm ready to have kids ...and more kids" because the purpose of this book is not to make people feel like they've lost their rights to have children it's simply to make people really consider carefully the decision to have and when to have children. Conscious "Pre-Parenting".

I'd like everyone to put thoughtfulness into the decision of bringing a child into this world. I offer a different point of view on parenting that will hopefully help shift the world's idea of the role of parenting all together.

This book will encourage people towards self-growth and looking deeper into their expectations and ideals around parenting. The goal for this book is to become a better prepared parent as well as look at some options on what to do when you are faced with unexpected parenting challenges.

My intention is not to discourage parenting as a matter of fact it's opposite as I feel that parenting is a blessing. And I'm not one of those fanatics that warn about over population either as I believe that the Earth is self-regulating, so if resources become limited then unfortunately people will just begin to starve and naturally reproduction will reduce but this is a very extreme view. I believe balance will always be restored by the universe. Unfortunately, the most over populated places will suffer the most until the Universe regulates itself.

I hope my story brings you growth.

CHAPTER TWO

My introduction to parenting

I first became pregnant at the age of 20. I was in University still in the beginning of my Psychology degree. This pregnancy resulted in a blighted ovum where the amniotic sack continued to grow but no baby developed within the sack, this always results in a miscarriage.

The confusion and hurt over my miscarriage left me very emotionally unstable. I left my boyfriend whom I still very much loved at the time, but feeling like a failure and not good enough to stay with him it was the best thing for both of us at the time. After this unpredictable experience and feeling a tremendous void I carelessly become pregnant again 6 months later to someone else, too soon to have fully grieved the loss of my previous pregnancy and the loss of my relationship.

I think somewhere in my mind I had hoped that the new pregnancy would help me get over my old relationship and the pregnancy I had just lost. Unfortunately, I carried my grief through my second pregnancy and into my new relationship. I just knew instinctively that my child was feeling that internal sadness I was still carrying.

I gave birth to my Virgo child at age of 22. But I wasn't the average 22-year-old, I was 22 going on 16 because I was so immature at the time and I felt as though my life had stopped evolving when I was 16 years old anyways due to my challenging childhood experiences.

After a traumatic birthing experience, I came to the realization that I had such a naive view of the world and of parenting in general. The parenting examples I had weren't the greatest after all. When the nurse handed me my Baby, a beautiful little girl. I looked at her in disbelief that "I" (very aware of my immaturity at this point) "a baby" had just given birth to "a baby". When the nurse was about to leave the room I said to her "Don't leave me alone with this baby, I don't know what to do with her" to which the nurse responded "Don't be silly you're the mother you'll figure it out!" Talk about a slap in the face. That's when reality hit me! I was now a mother but I didn't know how to be one. Apparently this is what my body was built for so I should just instinctually know what to do, right?

I had no experience around children! I had never held a baby before in my life much less changed a nappy or seen breastfeeding in person. I didn't have younger brothers or sisters only much older ones. I was the baby of the family and mostly seen but not heard I often rebelled in order to get attention. I didn't know how to be emotionally or physically responsible for a baby.

Those first few weeks were a struggle, lack of sleep, the pain of trying to establish breastfeeding when I had mastitis, living at home with my Mum who constantly made me feel as though I was doing everything wrong, not having my partner's help because we weren't living together and I didn't have a job.

After 4 weeks of painful breastfeeding I gave up on it which was hard as it was something I really wanted to continue doing but lacked the support. Every time I'd go to the maternity ward to ask for help they just said to give her the bottle. That was my first major feeling of failure as a Mother. My Virgo baby was not a good sleeper and was always unwell with ears, nose and throat problems. Months passed and I seemed to become more and more tired. The sadness within me continued to grow. I had dreamed of becoming a mother my whole life……so why was I feeling so dissatisfied and unhappy with this blessing I was given. Of course I was expecting that I was going to give birth to this quiet child that wouldn't cause me any work and do everything I wanted it to.

When my daughter reached one-year-old I bought an apartment by myself. Living on the single parent pension I continued to go about my life technically as a single parent with my daughter's Father only occasionally visiting on weekends. As time went on I began to lose my temper more and more with my child and my absent partner. There were days the sadness and exhaustion were so severe that I often contemplated taking my own life, wondering whether my daughter even deserved a Mother like me. Sometimes thinking if I could just go to sleep and never wake up I'd get some sort of rest and moment of relief. Secretly I was feeling so miserable, I resented my child for my not having finished my University degree, for my not being able to go out, for my life having no freedom to do simply daily things like going to the toilet, have a shower and sleeping without being interrupted constantly.

I was so depressed I would stay home for weeks at a time with closed curtains and not even having a shower most days. I began to get social anxiety and was too afraid to leave the house. If I knew I had to get out of the Car with my child I'd go into an anxiety attack. "What if she has a tantrum and people look at me like I'm a terrible Mother, what if she runs away, gets hit by a Car or I can't catch her then someone will steal my shopping?" these are some of the catastrophizing questions rolling around in my head at the time. My life felt stagnant and I saw very little into the future I just wanted to make it till the next day and in reality this is how I survived by just taking one day at a time.

I was lucky enough to have a couple of very amazing friends who worried about me. They all got together to organize a surprise Birthday Party for me and they combined enough money for me to buy some new clothes. One day they organized to watch my daughter while I went out to just do shopping for a few hours. One of them came with me to make sure I spent the money on myself and not on my child like I always did. I slowly started to realise how much emotional weight I put on top of my child as a reason for me to stay alive. Not only was I blaming my innocent girl for my life that I had chosen but I was expecting her to be the one to make me a happy person. To top it off I would even treat her bad and neglect her.

I eventually spoke to my doctor about what I was going through. Feeling very ashamed, I explained everything that I had been experiencing. I was diagnosed with Post Natal Depression as an extra on top of the Depression I had often felt in my life due to my childhood. I was put on Anti-depressants immediately. I suspected I might have been going through PND but had the fear that if I were to seek help that they would take my child away from me. In case you don't know here are some of the signs and symptoms of PND.

Signs of Postnatal depression

* Feeling down often and feeling doesn't seem to go away

* Feeling emotional and the need to cry all the time

* Feeling hopeless or like you are failing to meet your parenting expectations

* Worrying about the future and feeling powerless over your future.

* Feeling exhausted and physically unable to cope.

* Feeling anxious and panic sometimes without knowing why.

* Feeling anxiety around going out or being left alone with the child.

* Feeling excessive worry over the well-being of the baby.

* Feeling like you can't connect with the baby.

* Feelings of self-harm or fear that they might harm the baby.

* Feeling like you want to run away.

Years later came to learn that I had an extensive family history of Depression and some serious mental health conditions. I even had family members who had committed suicide. I was sad to learn that one of my Grandmothers was treated for depression with electric shock therapy. No one ever talked about it with me and I was too proud to ask or consider it as a possibility for me. Especially because I was studying Psychology. I believed that I should have known better simply because I studied the mind. But studies don't make you immune to depression.

I was on antidepressants for 1 year, determined to get better and get off them as soon as possible. I went back to studying to do a Diploma in Counselling. I had no intention of working in this field at this point I just wanted to find a way of fixing myself without medication. I wanted a better life and to become a better Mother to my Child, who clearly deserved better than what I had to offer at the time.

I came to learn a lot about PND through my studies as well as through my own experience. There are many theories for what may cause PND. It can be brought on by hormone imbalance, it can be the accumulation of stressful circumstances and/or environment, it can be brought on by accumulation of past events or challenging childhood and sometimes it's just simply the complication of having a challenging birth or baby. As there is no actual main conclusion to the cause of PND, for me,

I believe it was a combination of everything! I had a dysfunctional past plus my circumstances at the time of having a baby were unsettled plus the fluctuation of hormones plus not knowing what to do with a baby that was always unhappy and not sleeping as well (Don't forget that sleep deprivation can be a form of torture within interrogations) as well as the lack of support. It really was a recipe for disaster.

Studying Psychology and Counselling was a step in the right direction and beneficial but I still had much to learn and lots of hurdles to overcome.

CHAPTER THREE

Why do you want to have children?

Let's take a look at some common reasons why people choose to have children. Some may sound a little silly but you'll be surprised at some of the reasons I have heard. See if you can identify with some of these?

I want to have a child because:

"I feel like there's something missing in my life."

"I don't believe in abortion."

"I'm getting older and my biological clock is ticking"

"I'll receive a benefit from the government when I have a baby then I won't have to work."

"My partner really wants to have a baby and I really want to make my partner happy."

"It will save my marriage/relationship and then partner won't leave me."

"I just love babies and kids."

"People will respect me more as an adult if I have children."

"I'm financially ready."

"I want to pass down my family name."

"It's human nature and it's my right to have children."

"My other child needs a sibling."

"I'm lonely. My child will always love me unconditionally and always be a part of me."

"My children will take care of me when I get old."

"I've achieved my career it's just the next thing to do."

"It will be fun having children around the house."

"My breasts will get bigger during and after pregnancy."

"I'm married and that's the next thing to do."

"My partner is unwell and could die soon. I want to have a piece of him with me when he passes."

"I've always wanted a big family."

"My first labour was a traumatic experience out of my control and I want to prove that I can do it better this time."

Let's take a closer look at some of these reasons:

"I feel like there's something missing in my life."

Sometimes we feel a void like something is missing. It can be because we've lost someone close to us or maybe it's just a sense of not having a purpose in our lives. Regardless of what the cause of this feeling maybe it's easy to put the responsibility on someone else or an external source. In this particular case of choosing to have a child to fill the void the child would have to carry the weight and responsibility of filling that void within the parent. What happens if things then don't go as expected and the child is unable to fill the void? Is it then the child's fault for failing to make their parent happy?

I personally experienced this situation first hand. The sadness of the loss of my first pregnancy. I was hoping that my second pregnancy would fill the void of my first loss. So already, even before my child was born I had already placed a huge responsibility on her shoulders. It was her job to replace the child I had lost and her responsibility to make me happy. I was attached to the idea of what a child could give me. I was looking for unconditional love, connection and acceptance from a baby. I thought I'd finally have someone who would never leave me. When she was born I realised that it wasn't her job to unconditionally love me it was my job to just love her. I was still unhappy and with little love to give. I then blamed her for not being able to fill that void and make me happy. What a burden it must have been for my child to carry. The heavy burden of having to make me happy.

I would urge anyone who has this as an underlying reason for wanting to have children to look deeper. Why is it that makes you feel a void within you? Do you have unresolved childhood traumas or fear of abandonment? Are you needing more time to heal and grieve the loss of someone or something dear to you? Are there certain things in life that you wished you had done that you have not yet achieved?

When choosing to have a child it is best to feel as though your life is already complete. So that when you are considering to have a child they are just an addition to your life. You choose to have a child when you're so full of Love to give or let's say your glass is so full that you are ready to pour into another person's cup. This is called the spill-over effect. If your glass is almost empty or has very little to offer you are simply giving out what you don't have enough of within yourself.

Having children can be draining for the first few years. You want to make sure you are feeling strong, settled, self-fulfilled and balanced as much as possible before giving out so much of yourself to another human being. If you feel a void, fill that void within yourself first. You can't teach or give what you don't have.

"I don't believe in abortion."

Abortion should never be taken lightly and should not be looked at as a regular form of contraception. It's heartbreaking and a challenging decision for anyone to make.

For women – Termination of a pregnancy can be a traumatic event. When hormones and emotions automatically start to play a big role in the decision, It's common for women to make an emotionally influenced decision. The instinctual nature of a female is to protect the life that is growing inside her. This instinct rarely allows women to see beyond the pregnancy and all that it will take to raise a baby. Women can get caught up in the emotions and often decide to keep the baby.

However, if a woman was able to see past the emotional experience that is pregnancy and consider what may happen after the birth of the child a pregnancy termination can be considered with a more open mind. When a woman is able to ask herself questions such as is it the right time to have a baby? Am I emotionally balanced and stable enough to teach another human? Am I ready to have a baby right now? How does my partner feel about having a baby right now? Will my partner be there to support me? Are my finances in order and can I afford to have a child? Do I have a stable living arrangements? Have I achieved most of what I wanted to achieve before having children? Only when they've answered all these questions confidently then would a mindful decision be able to be made.

Spiritual or Religious influences in society can play a big role in the decision of whether to continue or terminate a pregnancy. Interestingly people who generally have no religious inclination at all normally, suddenly can become religious when they find out they are pregnant. Regardless it's important to consider what are your beliefs around the subject of Abortion? Are you a highly religious with the believe that God will punish you for terminating a pregnancy? Do you fear or worry about how people will see you or whether you'll be judged should you choose to terminate?

Many new age spiritualists believe that a soul is fully aware of the life that it chooses before it enters the physical world. If this is the case that would mean that before a soul animates an embryo it already knows that there is a chance that it will be aborted. That Soul chose to connect with that body prepared for this event to possibly take place. Maybe this was a karmic lesson or journey that soul signed up for intentionally or maybe it was a Karmic lesson for the mother.

A well know Medium in Australia, Anthony Grzelka writes in his book Medium Down Under as he compares the body to a form of transport. Anthony says "A Soul will have many options as to with who and where it is best-placed to achieve its learning experience. That is, which bus it needs to get onto that will best serve its purpose. The first option may not be available or in the case of a termination, no longer available. Guess what? No big deal! Another bus will be along that will suit that soul's purpose equally well. It's only our perceptions as physical beings that conjure up the idea that we have ended a life and that there is some major impact on the soul that wasn't born." The Spiritual view is that the Soul never dies.

Either way whatever choice is made all things should be considered. Emotions should be acknowledged, current life circumstances taken into consideration and personal beliefs need to be looked at in depth. Last thing you want to do is make a decision only to feel anguish or resentment afterwards. At the end of the day you want to look back and say that you made the decision that was best for you and all involved at the time. When you stand by your decision with conviction having weighed up the pros and cons it will avoid any feelings of guilt in the long run and you can look back respectfully at your decision.

Abortion when a disability is present

I thought I would add this extra section as unfortunately some parents are faced with the challenging decision of whether or not to terminate a pregnancy where a disability is present in the baby. In Australia it's illegal to terminate a pregnancy over 13 weeks old however there are other states within Australia which allow to terminate later if a disability is present. A doctor or local Women's support centre can offer better guidance on the locations where these terminations are available as I imagine this issue would vary around the world.

A Child is always a beautiful gift of life and deserves a chance at life like any other child regardless of whether it has a disability or not. Most disabled children have such a sweet innocent nature. They are to be treasured for the blessing that they are.

In a case where termination due to disability is considered it's important to look at a few aspects of this decision carefully. Let me clarify I'm talking about situations where the parent knows that there is a disability and chooses to keep a child anyways. I'm not talking about a situation where the parent didn't have a choice in the matter and where a child become disabled at birth. These circumstances are out of the parent's control.

A child with a disability is in constant need of extra time, assistance and attention. Therefore, caring for other children that are already in the family may become harder.

The lifespan of children with disabilities is often shorter than that of a healthy child. Consider how heartbreaking it would be for a parent to see their child pass before them. This usually seems against the natural order of things. In the chance that the disabled child does outlive the parent and the parent passes away first it's important to make plans to have people you entrust with the responsibility for looking after your disabled child. Ask the child's siblings, if they have any, if they are willing to take on the responsibility of looking after their disabled brother or sister. Make sure you are leaving your child in the trusted hands of someone who will love them as you did and look out for the best interests of your disabled child.

I realise this all sounds very blunt but I feel it's important to address some of these basics if "chosen" to continue a pregnancy knowing that the child is disabled. In general, we teach our children to survive and go about their own lives, but when it comes to children with a disability they will essentially never really be fully independent and we are naively expecting the world to love and accept them exactly the way we would as their parents. Then we leave them behind hoping society will just take care of them. Unfortunately, this isn't always the case.

Whether you choose to terminate this pregnancy or not regardless Please seek as much support, information and assistance as possible.

"I'm getting older and my biological clock is ticking."

Addressing the subject that increasing age will dramatically reduce your fertility can be a very valid reason for hurrying the process. However, take a good look at other options such as freezing your eggs to buy you a little more time. In reality by the time your body has completely stopped producing eggs you may be reaching an age where actually having a child isn't on your priority list.

Look over your life carefully and consider all the reasons both positive and negative as to why you have waited so long to have children. You may find yourself gaining some clarity as to why you haven't yet chosen to have children. Consider whether the circumstances in your life have changed and what is different now? Why would having a child now be any different to having had a child back then? Weigh up the pros and cons.

"I'll receive a benefit from the government when I have a baby then I won't have to work."

A child should not be a means to financial security. In countries with great government incentives and benefits it's common for especially teens and young women to fall into the thinking that if they have a child they'll be financially set.

A Child is not a prize or a medal you wear. A child is not a means of financial security in fact it's quite the opposite. Children have basic needs such as food, drink shelter, clothing, education and medication. If they're lucky enough they'll also have some extra hobbies such as sport, music or art which their parents would be happy to pay for.

For those thinking that having a child is an easy stay at home job they will be hard done by to find that having a child is worth 2 full time jobs. There's no clock o button. It takes a village to do what an efficient mother does on a daily basis.

In the end what happens when the child is old enough to go about their independent lives and those government benefits stop. What will the parent be left to fall onto financially? Especially if they have been out of the workforce for so long, returning to work in an ever changing society is challenging with little up to date life skills.

"My partner really wants to have a baby" and "It will save my marriage/relationship."

Similar to the first reasons around filling a void, this touches upon the subject of putting the responsibility on top of the child to make someone happy.

Beware of a relationship reliant on a child to become a better relationship. If a relationship is not stable and balanced without a child how will a child make it stable and balanced? Quite the opposite actually. A child will throw into the mix bigger challenges to face within the relationship. If for some unfortunate reason the marriage fails, then is it the child's fault because the child failed to keep the relationship together. This is a big burden to carry. If it's the child's responsibility to keep the parents connected, then the child controls the household and the relationship. This can cause all sorts of other parenting challenges. Eventually when the child becomes independent the parents are faced once again with time alone with each other and needing to find ways to reconnect without the child being the buffer.

I recommend reading two amazing books "How to improve your marriage without talking about it." by Patricia Love and Steven Stosny and "What children learn from their parent's marriage." by Judith P. Siegel.

Children look up to their parents as an example. Your relationship with your partner is your child's first exposure and example to what a relationship is supposed to look like and how it is supposed to function. Whatever you do, your child will think it's normal. When they grow up their household, relationships are their first point of reference for future relationships. The influence of the parental relationship with each other will greatly shape their own relationships in the future. So it's important to make sure they're given the best example possible. It's their blueprint for life.

Something that's also worth mentioning that no one will ever verbalise to you is if the relationship does break down and your partner finds someone else, just remember that your child will be sleeping between your partner and the new step parent. This can be a tough pill to swallow for some people, knowing that a new person has now stepped into your life or parenting role.

So be very VERY sure about the person you choose to have children with. Make sure you can see yourself with them long term and possibly growing old with them. This doesn't mean you have to stay in an unhappy marriage it just means you made the decision with long term in mind not short term gains.

> **"People will respect me more as an adult if I have children."**

Unfortunately, we would like to believe that child will raise our respect lever, social status or Heir achy within our home. Teenagers tend to fall into this way of thinking more often. When they have to go home and live with their parents as a parent themselves they realise that they are still not the respected or the boss of their own children. Especially if they are having to live at home with their own mum or dad, at home they are still the child not the parent!

This can be a very challenging environment to live in simply because the new mum is trying to parent while they are still being mothered themselves by their own mother. This was a challenge I also faced with my first child. The baby grows up noticing that their mother actually isn't the boss in the house and looks to the grandparent as the authoritative figure. As you can imagine this causes quite a bit of conflict with everyone trying to fight for power and recognition. It takes a very mature household to cope in a situation like this.

"My child needs a sibling."

Children are very adaptable generally whatever situation they are exposed to they will think is normal. It's their natural instinct is to adjust to any changes within the household. To put the responsibility of needing to have more children on a child themselves can be a big asking.

A child doesn't know whether you have the stability, extra finances, extra time, extra space or extra love for that matter. And what happens when they find out they can't send their brother or sister back to where it came from when their sibling is not fulfilling a need they were searching for to be met?

"I'm lonely. A child will always love me unconditionally and always be a part of me" and "My children will take care of me when I get old."

While children offer us the opportunity to "experience" unconditional love they give very little by way of help, support, affection or appreciation for the first few years of their life. I've often heard mums say that they give give give and get nothing in return. The most common complaint is feeling extremely unappreciated.

It's important to keep in mind that it's the responsibility of the parent to love themselves and make themselves happy, not the child. The parent must teach the child how to love and take care of themselves by way of example. If the child sees that the parent is unable to take care of their own needs. The child will be forever searching for happiness outside of themselves. A goal which will forever feel out of reach.

Being a parent really is such a humbling experience. As a parent we give love endlessly. To expect a child to take responsibility for the parent seems slightly opposite to the natural cycle of life. As a parent you do it because it's your responsibility. As for a child when they grow up and become independent beings they simply take care of the parent out of choice. As a parent you have to accept that they may very likely not want to take on that responsibility.

"I'm married and that's the next thing to do."

I feel that this subject needs to be looked at brie y because it's important that each couple recognises that not every couple has to be the same. If you and your partner don't feel that parenting is the right step for both of you then you aren't doing your child or your personal life any justice by bringing a child into the world for the sake of society's expectation.

"I just love babies and kids"

Get a job in a childcare!! If taking care of children is something you love to do on a daily basis, why not get paid to do it. You can do this for the rest of your life and don't have to worry about them growing up because you will always have more of someone else's kids to look after. This way you don't have to be constantly responsible for all of those children you can actually hand them back to their parents at the end of the day. Win Win situation!

CHAPTER FOUR

From bad parenting to conscious parenting

When I was 25 years old my father had an aneurism (my daughter was nearly 3 years old), causing him serious brain damage. My Dad was no longer the same person for the remainder of his living years and I felt like I had lost my best friend. This became another big down turn in my life. My father and I were very close. I began to have regular anxiety and panic attacks, feeling guilty that I couldn't take care of him and just didn't know how to cope with that. It was horrible to watch him deteriorate. A man that was strong as a Bull and so loved and respected by all his friends was left abandoned. I would occasionally hide in my closet in the dark to cry. When my daughter would find me crying she would sit quietly beside me and rub my back to comfort me.

I found it hard to function as a mother when my father became ill. I was always getting angry and would have emotional outbursts that would scare my daughter. There were mornings I couldn't get out of bed to function properly (May I note my daughter didn't sleep a full night until she was 5 years old). My Virgo was an early bird and would go watch TV quietly too afraid to wake me up in the morning so I wouldn't lose my temper.

One morning she burnt her hand on the toaster trying to make me breakfast in bed. She wrapped her hand in a tea towel to hide the burn knowing that I would get angry at her for touching the toaster unsupervised.

I remember once going to a shopping centre after a night of little sleep as usual in absolute exhaustion trying to do food shopping with my Virgo, she was annoying me asking for some lollies or something and I yelled at her to "stop following me and leave me alone". I don't know what I was thinking, where would she go? Was I stupid or something? I must have been losing my mind.

I did and said things at times that I find hard to reiterate without crying. Perhaps the most horrible thing I did to my child was threatening her with a knife. One image that will never leave my mind is the fear on her face. I can't imagine the trauma this caused her. When I tried to talk to her about the incident years later she didn't remember anything. I assume the trauma must have been so much so that she completely repressed it and lost that piece of her memory. Nevertheless, I've been apologising for it ever since, knowing that this will never erase the event for her.

Guilt is the hardest internal pain to bare.

She was such a clingy child, she wanted so much to be loved by me, internally I just had so little to offer. Sometimes I think I just didn't have the emotional capacity to love another human being as I was just so miserable and angry within myself since I was a teenager. It became unbearable to see how emotionally responsible my child had become for me.

When my Virgo was closely approaching three years old I finally heeded the advice of a friend and put her in childcare

2-3 days a week so I could occasionally leave the house, have some time for myself and sleep. I would occasionally clean houses for some extra money when I could. Every dirty toilet I cleaned I would start crying and saying to myself "I can do so much more than this." I knew I had to make changes and that's what I was determined to do.

I separated from my daughter's father when she was around three years old. When my daughter turned four I sold my home and moved far from where I was living at the time hoping to start fresh in a new location. I travelled to my homeland, Portugal, to visit my barely functioning Father before something should happen and he pass away. I paid off my car and studies and put my 100% focus on my Counselling studies and healing myself.

Through my studies I began to take a deep look at myself and my personal conditioning and belief systems. Becoming a parent brought up all my past hurts around my parent's separations and dysfunctional relationships. Both my parents had been marriage and divorced 3 times each. I became even more determined to break the cycle. I didn't want my daughter to learn or think that my family patterns where encouraged or normal. That's when my intense "Inner child work" started.

I completed various courses within Counselling, Psychotherapy and Child Development. In the hope that I would be "fixed" I worked on myself with relentless self-discipline and tireless determination, I step by step became more patient and caring towards my daughter's needs. By this time my daughter was around five years old unfortunately so much emotional damage had already been done. Sometimes I would lift my arms to hug my Virgo child and she would flinch and put her hands over her head as if she was protecting herself from me, thinking that I was going to hit her or something. It took me a long time to convince her that I wasn't going to hurt her anymore, especially after I had already hurt her for so long. All those years of bad parenting were not going to be a quick fix and I would forever hold the remorse of having wasted so many years with my child that we could have been close.

It wasn't a process that happened over night but one day at a time, one week at a time, one month at a time. I began to shift and to notice my emotional outbursts become less and less common. My Virgo slowly began to trust me and I did more and more things with her. Mother and daughter time become a big priority to me. I knew I wasn't a great mother but my first step was just to become a more conscious mother. Just having that extra awareness for now was my main goal. I occasionally started dating again but Men were very low priority over my mother-daughter relationship. Being back in the dating game as a Mother was a scary experience for me. Who would want a Woman with a child I thought, and how will I know if they will be good to my child? Can I trust anyone?

What is this world coming to?

I experienced first-hand a very violent attack on a neighbour that shook me tremendously. I was living in a small unit at the time in a very rough neighbourhood as that's all I could afford to buy at the time. I woke up to the horrifying screams of a 2-year-old child. "Mummy, Mummy!" repeatedly over and over again with screams and shaking tremors mixed in the words. Then came the bangs, smashing of windows and a male aggressive voice. I opened my door and left my security door locked to see what was happening. A mother was holding her little toddler curled around him to shield him while a man was beating her as she was trying to get away. He beat her all the way out of the house and I saw her fall down the stairs holding her child, the child's screams getting more and more panicked. I had already called the police earlier to alert them when I first heard the child's screams but didn't know to what extent of what was going on and had kept them on the phone to hear what was happening. I began to scream as loud as I could at my front door with the security door still locked "Help, Help Someone call the police!" This was enough to scare the man who was beating this Women to run away. For a few moments I was too terrified to open the door fearing for my safety and the safety of my child who was in bed and unaware of what was going on at the time.

Once things seemed clear I ran out to help the woman and child. She was beaten so badly she could barely talk and her toddler was huddled over her still yelling at her "mummy mummy!" to see if she was still alive. Finally, the police arrived with the ambulance and took care of her I think I still had the phone call in my hand active.

The next day she came and knocked on my door to thank me. She insisted that I saved her life. Apparently she had gone to a party earlier and had met a man who she had rejected, so this man proceeded to follow her home and got very angry at her rejection. What is this world coming to when a man feels so much need to do something like this? She showed me all her bruises on her back and chest it was like someone had painted her body black. I was just so thankful that the child was ok.

For years I was haunted by this child's screams. I would occasionally wake up in the night and think I was still hearing it. Things like this happen in the movies I thought not in real life, It's something I never want to experience again. This experience opened another door for me cognitively, I felt an even bigger compassion towards children and respect for their loyalty and fragility. Children trust us as "big people" to protect them! These events are things no child should ever have to experience.

CHAPTER FIVE

Parenting styles

So now that we have established all the reasoning and motivations behind our desire to become parents let's have a look at the type of parents we'd like to become and the legacy we'd like to pass down to our children.

Before I had children I noticed how strong my opinions were around parenting. I used to see badly behaved children and blame their parents for lack of discipline. I used to judge parents when their kids were dirty or cold and had no shoes on. I would judge mothers who didn't take care of themselves and beauty needs I thought "Oh I'd never let myself go that way when I have kids" and when mothers had a dirty house I'd think what does this woman do all day. I would judge parents for not making "mummy and daddy time" to be together without the kids. OH BOY WAS I NAIVE!!

What I found out is that our biggest mistakes are made with our first child. That's when all hidden beliefs and suppressed childhood fears come up. The things you were exposed to as a child come up like an autopilot re ex. Those exact things you swore you wouldn't do to your children you begin to do, simply because you don't know any different and that's the only conditioning that you have. Here lies the first hurdle, what kind of parent would you like to become? Did you agree with the way you're your parents raised you? How do you and your partner differ on parenting opinions? or agree on how you would like to parent your children? Here are common Parenting Styles:

1. **Authoritarian Parenting**

This parenting style is a very restrictive with often heavy punishment children must follow directions with little or no explanation. Punishment often involves screaming and smacking when the child misbehaves. These parents often see the world as a hostile unsafe place to live and try to discipline and train their children to survive in an unforgiving aggressive society. When the child of this parent questions reasoning for parent's ideals the child is often met with the response of "Because I said so"

2. **Authoritative Parenting**

This style holds high expectations of maturity from the child. Authoritative parents encourage their children to be independent but still place limits on their actions. These parents are understanding and responsive to their children and teach them how to regulate their feelings and emotions through communication skills. When children fail to meet the authoritative parent's expectations these parents are more forgiving and nurturing rather than punishing. They want their children to have the natural ability to confidently and assertively sort out their own problems and co-operate within society.

3. **Permissive/Indulgent Parenting**

Permissive Parents make very little demands of their children. They don't expect their children to have a huge amount of self-control or maturity for this reason rarely discipline. They understand that their children are simply passing through their necessary phases of growth. These parents communicate well sometimes holding very little information back, often becoming more like a friend rather than a parent.

4. Neglectful/Uninvolved Parenting

These parents are very detached uninvolved, unresponsive, cold and neglectful. The lack of emotional support and encouragement creates a discouraging environment for the child. This can occur if the parent is feeling unsupported and has a lack of resources themselves. While they may still be able to meet the basic needs of the child such as food, shelter and clothing they are unable to connect with their child on a deeper level

Some more modern parenting styles are:

Attachment Parenting

Also known as natural parenting is based on the parent focusing on building a strong, trusting, empathic relationship with your children by responding sensitively and promptly to the child's emotional and physical needs. There is no specific set of rules for this type of parenting as the parent is guided by the child's needs at the time. This involves responding to your baby's cries immediately;

demand breastfeeding for an extended periods of time; carrying or wearing your baby as often as possible; using gentle ways to help your baby sleep; co-sleeping with your baby and minimising separation from your baby during the first few years of life.

Following into the later years this parenting style provides an understanding, loving and nurturing environment for the child to feel free and safe enough to express themselves. Their natural talents and abilities are recognised and nourished at an early age. This develops the child's sensitivity towards themselves and others.

Hover parenting or Helicopter Parenting

A helicopter parent is a parent who pays extremely close attention to a child's or children's experiences and problems, particularly at educational institutions. Helicopter parents are named so because, like helicopters, they hover overhead, overseeing their child's life constantly. This is a very controlling form of parenting.

Hand in Hand parenting

Listening with respect to your child and model the behaviours you wish to teach and nurture within your child. Using your intuition and creativity to solve problems. Create relationships by connecting the "whole" family compassionately with warmth and trust. Creating balance in home and work like. Reinforces openness, acceptance and willingness to confront issues together as a family. Most importantly having appreciation for individual qualities within a family.

Spiritual Parenting

Teaching the child about God or a Source of Energy from which we were all created. Spiritual parenting teaches about the oneness and connectedness of all mankind. It teaches that we are the creators of our reality and we are a part of the Creator therefore making us ourselves also creators. Spiritual parents find the magic and miracle in each moment. They teach presence and reinforce "The power of Now" concept (Eckhart Tolle). Spiritual parenting is being in complete acceptance of what is. There is no resistance to life and what is happening, one simply just trusts that what is happening is what needs to happen.

When a good emotion or a bad emotion comes to the surface the children are taught to observe these emotions without judgement in order to embrace their "Shadow" aspects of self as well as their positive aspects of self. Either way there is no right or wrong there is merely self and the movement towards what feels best for each individual self.

What's your conditioned parenting style?

Did you pick up on your parent's parenting style? Becoming aware of your conditioning will give you a heads up about your internal belief system. Looking at this more deeply you can begin to work on making the changes to adapt or create a parenting style that is best suited to your personality. There is no right or wrong there's just the experience that you are wanting to have.

I remember once asking a dear friend who hadn't yet had any children and was closely approaching 40, if she was considering ever having children? Her response to me was "Why would I bring a child into this world if I'm so screwed up already myself. Why would I screw up another person's life?" Her wisdom and understanding of the impact that her own state of mind could make on another human being really made me think. If only everyone, including me had this kind of wisdom before having had children.

The missing link within parenting styles

In a world that has so much inconsistency within parenting styles and views I believe that the most important thing to teach your children is "Your freedom ends where mine begins, and my freedom ends where yours begins" A child has every right to express themselves as long as that expression of themselves is not hurting another human being. A child has a right to try different things as long as it doesn't put anyone else's life at risk. A child has a right to freedom as long as their freedom doesn't impede on someone else's freedom. It's really quite that simple. This concept can be implemented in almost every situation of life. All that needs to be done is ask yourself "Am I hurting or going to hurt anyone by choosing to do what I am about to do?"

I feel that this is the missing link within all extremes of parenting. There are children who have excessive amount of freedom to the point of where their parents care little about what their children do, where they go or how they treat other people. On the other side of the spectrum there are children who are so trapped and wrapped in cotton wool, without being allowed to speak. They don't even know what freedom is and as a result lack initiative or a sense of self. By teaching the "My freedom ends where yours begins" rule parents can create a happy medium between these two parenting extremes. A parent can remain an influential part of a child's life taking on the co-creator role while still allowing the child freedom to find and express themselves safely, without being a problem to society. Only a beneficial, respectful addition to society.

There's a common misconception that giving children more freedom will turn them into selfish, self-centred people that will go around stealing and killing as they wish. This is simply not true. Have you ever seen a happy person go and kill someone? Have you ever seen someone who has always had enough food and never had to worry about a lack of food go and steal food from someone? It's simply not going to happen. If children are taught that what they want is OK and that they have a right to have what they want and are shown ways to get what they want in a healthy way that is not hurting anyone else, they are unlikely to become a selfish forceful burden on society as they will feel no need to take from others.

CHAPTER SIX
Healing through my studies and experiences

I journeyed endlessly through my Counselling, Psychotherapy and Child Development studies, hoping to gain knowledge, maturity and Consciousness. I did my majors in Dysfunctional Family Counselling, Marriage and Relationship Counselling and Conflict Resolution. Step by step I moved towards the Woman and Mother I always wanted to become. I was able to step back and look at my child as the sweet innocent soul that she was. Re-parenting my "inner child" taught me to have love and compassion towards not only myself whom I had neglected for so long but to have love and compassion for all children.

I began to understand that children are just processing things in a different, more sensory way and at a slower rate than I. Sometimes we explain things to children expecting them to just get it immediately but in all honesty we really need to give them a few extra seconds or sometimes minutes to process our instructions.

When we are hurrying them into the car, our sense of urgency is based on our own agenda and needs because according to them they don't really know where they are meant to be or what they are meant to be doing. They have no sense of time or responsibility. They are simply counting on you to know what comes next.

I experimented with different techniques that helped me cope with daily chores and necessities on a daily basis. Jo Frost well known as the Super Nanny has some amazing ideas in her videos on how to encourage your children to do things without causing damage to their self-esteem. I highly recommend all Jo Frost's books.

Interestingly though the more I studied and learnt how to do numerous techniques on a daily basis with regards to routines and good parenting skills I still felt like there was a small piece of the puzzle missing. Like a missing link. I felt myself moving closer towards my purpose in life but I wasn't quite there yet. It was at this stage that I became open to the idea of actually using my Counselling studies and experiences towards helping people in the future, but still wasn't ready. I knew I wanted to save every child from having to experience a Mother like me I just wasn't sure at this stage how to do that.

I did the government funded Parentlink volunteering course and became a home visitor volunteer for CLAN This home visiting service helps parents with basic routines, child development and disciplinary concerns. This course was amazing! Very practical and informative. It allowed us Volunteers to work on ourselves on a deeper level and it didn't automatically guarantee placement with a family. You had to be competent enough to do the job. By this time, I was. ☺

My confidence within my parenting skills grew. Having overcome my challenges, I became better able to support women going through so many similar challenges that I had gone through. It surprised me to see just how many Women out there were suffering silently, yet all telling the exact same stories. I think it was at this point in my life that I knew I would one day write a book that would hopefully touch the hearts of all Women and give them hope for a better parenting experience.

I got the opportunity to do some Admin work for the Department of Child Protection. This was one of the most challenging things I've ever had to do in my life. I got to see how things worked within the Department. It was such a stressful environment. The workers were overloaded with cases. There was policy after policy that needed to be acknowledged before any action was taken within a family… And when action was taken it was unavoidably traumatising to witness.

Children were being mistreated or abused and being removed from their parents or home. But the most disturbing thing to me was the way these children would cling onto their abuser! It struck me time and time again that these children who were being mistreated had no clue that there was anything wrong with the way they were living or being treated. To them what they were experiencing was absolutely normal and unquestionable. They didn't know any different and all that they suffered they thought to be just simply the way it was in the world.

So the minute someone tried to remove them from an abusive environment they would fight tooth and nail to stay where they were. Simply because they don't know any different and they especially couldn't possibly imagine a life any better than what they have only come to know.

Working at the Department was a real eye opener. Stories emerged about children being handcuffed to their beds for days not being given food or opportunities to go to the toilet. When found in their rooms were weak, sun deprived and food deprived in a room full of poo and smell of urine. Babies were being neglected left in their cots and dying with failure to thrive, babies and young kids being sexually abused as young as 8 months old. Mother's suffering from such serious depression accused of harming or attempting to drown their children. So many of these stories where more common that you would think. Any of the challenges I faced growing up paled in comparison to the things some of these children were being exposed to. For a small moment I almost felt like what I had done wasn't so bad, ALMOST!

The repeating question within me was "Why and how can people treat children this way?" My compassion for children reached a level beyond I had ever imagined it could. I began to respect these little beings for their flexibility, strength, openness and tolerance for what they suffered in the hands of adults who really had no common sense to know any better. Even though they are so small and fragile children place all their trust in adults to take care of their wellbeing. When Children are abused they don't ask questions they simply adapt, survive through it and keep moving forward. Most of the times still with a smile on their face to offer. The day I left the Department I promised myself that I would find a way to reach out and touch as many parents as possible. I realise it's a big ask for one person but I figured if I wrote a book and spread the word maybe I could touch as many people as I could and create changes to save children from heartache in the hands of adults.

With all of this going on I still wasn't sure what my role was going to be in all this. What was I going to do for work? What would I be known as? as a parent support worker? a Counsellor? another super nanny or baby whisperer? None of these titles seemed to fit what I was really wanting to do. In reality I just wanted to give Mother's a heads up, but most importantly teach them to know when to ask for help.

CHAPTER SEVEN
Can you prepare yourself for parenting?

To a certain extent yes! What's the main difference between people who can have children naturally and people who need to plan their parenting experience such as gay couples, people with fertility conditions and those who can't have children biologically themselves for other unknown reasons? The difference is that people who cannot have children naturally need to put a lot more thought and preparation into the decision.

When there is a medical reason for why a couple is unable to have children fertility clinics and doctors are extensively involved, expensive medications and lab costs not to mention the time involved and physical and emotional stress on the couple going through fertility treatments. There are failed implantations, preparing for a child only to find out the treatment was unsuccessful and more. For Gay couples wishing to adopt everything is taken into consideration. Departments look into the security of the couple's financial status, stability within the couple's relationship, the condition of the household and whether it is safe and child friendly, whether it will be a two parent or single parent home and whether these parents have a previous criminal record. I've only touched the tip of the iceberg.

If all of these things need to be taken into consideration with couples who can't have children naturally is it fair that those who can have children naturally can do so without needing to consider all the same things other couples have to before having children? Simply because a couple can get pregnant naturally doesn't mean they shouldn't look deeper into their own circumstances to see if they are truly ready to support another human being or more of them.

Unplanned pregnancies are becoming more and more common. People are labelling their children as "the accident". Let's face it if you're having sex there's always a risk of pregnancy. I'm not talking about those who took full precautions, used protection, contraception or were victims of rape and got pregnant, I'm talking about those who were careless (like me with my first child) and pretend to ignore the risk of pregnancy when having unprotected sex. Then act surprised when they or their partner get pregnant.

As Humans need to take responsibility for our actions and take into consideration all lives involved in our decisions.

It would be a more pleasant experience to sit down with your partner and decide on a time to start having children? Choosing a time in your life where life is calm, stable and settled? Having the pleasure of the love making with the purpose of creating another life out of love and connection? Having that child come into the world wanted and with the feeling of the love between two people. From the beginning this creates a more encouraging, welcoming and supportive environment for the child to come into. Having the best beginnings will help smooth the way for the unplanned challenges that we are all faced with when having children.

When having children, you will be confronted with many extra challenges such as gaining knowledge of your own suppressed childhood emotions and finding out you have more triggers than you thought. Children have a way of learning all the right buttons to push within their parents to get a rise out of them. Being a parent raises heaps of opportunities to do a lot of "Inner child work" and "Shadow Work". Inner child work involves therapy that looks deeper into suppressed emotions and unhealed aspects of yourself that were left unresolved as a child. Sometimes we aren't even aware of these suppressed aspects of ourselves till our children cause a trigger within us to go off. Inner child therapy is great where childhood trauma has occurred. Sometimes we have post traumatic stresses that we didn't even know we had because we've simply dissociated ourselves with that aspect of our life. Trust me when you have children all of these unhealed issues come back up for the opportunity to be healed.

Similarly, shadow work involves integrating negative aspects of yourself that have been suppressed due to blaming or shaming as a child. Shadow work helps us to accept negative aspects of ourselves, so by learning to accept our faults and all, we are more likely to be accepting of our own children's faults. I highly recommend both of therapies before having children. I will explain these in slightly more detail later in this book. Both these therapies require a person to be very open minded and willingness to take full responsibility for their actions and thoughts.

However, find a therapy that helps you integrate and accept every part of your being, both positive and negative. Learning about how you would have liked to be treated as a child, how to deal with your emotions and accept yourself as you are will give you big tools and a big advantage over your parenting experience. Not only will you be able to remain emotionally stable for your child when your child needs you most but you will be less likely to take out your own emotions on your child and make them responsible for your feelings and triggers.

Other ways to prepare for parenting is to sit down with your partner and discuss your parenting goals and beliefs. Find common ground on what and how you would like to raise your children and what's important to you to teach them. Do you believe in punishment and reward? How will the finances be handled? Who will go to work and who will look after the kids? If a situation arises where you can't agree how will you both deal with the difference in opinion? Even simple things like routines should be discussed such as what time do you believe kids should go to bed and will you have Mummy and Daddy alone time before bed. Look at whether you believe children should self soothe alone in their bed or do you both agree that falling asleep with an adult is more comforting. Take in to consideration cultural beliefs also if both parents are not from the same culture. For example, do you believe your children to give a kiss on both cheeks to greet people, each time they wake up or come home. It might sound silly but raising and discussing some of these beliefs puts everyone on the same page and may avoid some future arguments.

The Importance of balance between Masculine and Feminine energy

Everyone has aspects of Masculine and Feminine within them. Both are needed in order to create balance. The Yin and Yang "together" make a whole. The essential aspects of feminine energy are associated with creation, birth, changes, nurturing, healing, receptivity, love, openness, understanding, compassion, emotions and intuition. The essential aspects of Masculine energy are associated with action, responsibility, protection, security, generosity, support, motivation, material abundance, strength, clarity and focus.

I mention this because of the importance that both the Masculine and Feminine role play within the raising of a child. I'm not necessarily saying that every child needs a Mother and a Father as there are families that have two Mums or two Dads and so many variations in between. What I'm referring to is the importance of the exposure to both the Feminine and Masculine energies within the guardians or mentors. Couples with two Mum's generally have one parent that has an inclination towards more of a feminine way of being and the other towards a more masculine way of being and same goes for a couple with two dads'. As a single Mum it's more challenging but I often hear Mum's say they have to play both roles but they just end up stressed out trying to play both at the same time.

It's important that children are exposed to both aspects of energy so that they learn to integrate both aspects of Masculine and Feminine within themselves and harmonise and accept both positive and negative qualities of Masculine and Feminine. Having both Mother and

Father figure in their lives can be highly beneficial to creating internal balance.

For example, a child may need to discuss an emotional issue involving the heart. A child that has both masculine and feminine influences will know that they might get a more nurturing and compassionate point of view from the feminine dominant energy and they might get a more practical, strategic approach from the masculine dominant energy. Neither are right or wrong both are just different perspectives. However, a child with only one parent let's say with only a masculine dominant energy they will only be exposed to one aspect or way of looking at the world. Therefore, that child may have less variety on course of actions to take towards their daily challenges due to having being exposed to only a limited perspective.

So whenever possible opting to having two parents will always be beneficial. If this is unavoidable and for example you are the Feminine dominant energy raising the child try and find ways to expose your child to some positive Masculine roles and/or Male figures that will awaken their other aspects of self within your child and vice versa if you are a Masculine figure raising a child. Your child will only bene t from having a more open minded way of looking at the world through Masculine and Feminine glasses.

Some Extras to prepare you:

Another helpful tip on how to prepare for parenting is to find ways to make yourself a happy, more calm person internally. I recommend practicing meditation, yoga or anything that will enhance awareness and presence. When your children are pushing your buttons and you're finding it hard to stay calm the ability to remain centred and present will be your most valued tool.

Research about how to become an Authentic version of yourself. These days many people are living in a way that is appropriate to society's expectations of them. Either because they were shamed as a child, taught to hold in their emotions and not express them or just simply shown by example through mentors how they need to act in order to manipulate what they want out of others, e.g.: being false or charming to get their way.

Authenticity within a person is a quality that should be valued. Knowing exactly who you are and what the truth is for you is essential when trying to teach a child how to be their own Authentic self and trust in their own truth.

Can you think of a time when you did or said something when you really wanted to actually do or say something else that felt more internally true to who you are? But you didn't out of fear of judgement? Was there a time when you ignored your inner voice that urged you to be honest? Or a time when you told someone one thing to their face and said something completely different behind their back? I realise there are certain situations where you're not always going to be able to be completely forthcoming to avoid conflict, however, minimising the necessity to do this will avoid a lot of internal entrapment, suppression and resentment. The feeling of constantly having to hold in what you really feel is enough to literally make your body deteriorate from the inside out. This is how cancers are formed.

There are some amazing self-help and consciousness enhancing books out there. I recommend all parents read some of these books or even download some audio books if they don't have time to sit down and read. I would often put my earphones on and listen to my audio books while I was doing my housework.

Here is a list of some of my favourite books. I recommend these not only to prepare you for parenting but also for your own personal growth. Please don't ever stop searching for ways to grow.

- A New Earth - Eckhart Tolle
- Nonviolent Communication: A Language of Life - Marshall B. Rosenberg
- What Children Learn from Their Parents' Marriage - Judith P. Siegel
- The Five Love Languages - Gary Chapman
- When Your Kids Push Your Buttons, and What You Can Do About It – Bonnie Harris
- Mommy Man - Jerry Mahoney
- Emotional Intelligence - Daniel Goleman
- Biology of Belief - Bruce H. Lipton
- Power Vs Force - David R. Hawkins
- The Completion Process - Teal Swan
- Raising the Spirited Child - Mary Sheedy Kurcinka
- Confident Parents Remarkable Kids - Bonnie Harris

- How To Talk So Kids Will Listen and Listen So Kids Will Talk - Adele Faber & Elaine Mazlish

- A Pace of Grace: The Virtues of a Sustainable Life – Linda Kavelin Popov

- Being Zen - Ezra Bayda

- Depression and Your Child - Deborah Serani

- Indigo, Crystal and Rainbow Children - Doreen Virtue

- Why Good People Do Bad Things - Debbie Ford

- The Woman Code - Sophia A. Nelson

- Supernanny – How to Get The Best From Your Children - Jo Frost

- Shame and Pride – Donald L Nathanson

Spend as much time with other people's children as possible. If you have a kind trusting friend that's willing to let you babysit as much as possible maybe even spend a week with their children so you can get an idea of what it's like to have children around you constantly on a daily basis. Tackle as many daily chores as possible while looking after a baby. This is great hands on experience!

I want to mention that I always enjoyed watching episodes of The Dog Whisperer with Caesar Milan. By no means am I telling people to raise their children like dogs! However, I can't go past some of the interesting ideas that Caesar has around working with the natural instinctual energy of animals. Children are also very instinctual and have a strong connection with animals for this reason. Sometimes watching the body language of animals can sometimes be similar to children. for example, when Dogs avoid eye contact and turn away they are unwilling to engage and children do the same.

Children become socialised into an adult society and as adults we teach them to lose those instinctual qualities such as showing dislike towards someone they don't feel comfortable around simple because we think its polite to say hello and smile at everyone. Caesar teaches how to bring about balance through regular exercise and play and how to tone down anxiety by projecting calm and confident energy. Most of what he teaches can be applied to parenting. Confident calm parents who spend time doing regular activities with their children are more likely to have calmer confident more well behaved children who are able to follow instructions.

Caesar also addresses the concept that the difference between humans and animals is the thought gap or space between a stimulus and your reaction to that stimulus. Within Animals when something happens to them they act instinctually. Whereas Humans we have brief gap or space of time between to gather our emotions and thoughts to choose what we are going to do about the situation.

The trick to becoming a more conscious human is to work on increasing that brief gap between Action-Reaction in order to make better decisions. A good example of this is when your child has done something naughty rather than instinctually smacking them use your human ability to use that little thinking gap to calm down and find a more appropriate course of action to take. This way rather than you being controlled by what triggered you, you are actually in control of the situation. I can't say how beneficial this advice has been for me not only within parenting but within my daily life.

So! can you prepare yourself for parenting? I believe you can, at least provide a good foundation from the beginning. All this information doesn't guarantee that you will be the perfect parent simply because the perfect parent doesn't exist. Just like the perfect child and the perfect family doesn't exist. However, knowing and putting into practice all this information can provide better beginnings and better chances at being successful. Understand that parenting is a growth enhancing experience. Parenting will offer you the opportunity for personal expansion and growth. Give yourself the best chances possible to get it right from the very start.

CHAPTER EIGHT

Postnatal Depression take two!

I met my husband when my first child was nearly six years old. Once again I was careless and I had an unplanned pregnancy very early on in this relationship. For numerous reasons it wasn't the right time for us to have a child together. We felt this way because he was living overseas at the time and I wasn't prepared to go back to being a single Mum with two children. We were in a new relationship, still getting to know each other and I hadn't yet settled within my career. Finances were scarce and we both had children from previous marriages to also consider.

Even though I was completely against abortion at the time, I felt that bringing a child into this kind of unstable environment could have caused more emotional damage to everyone involved long term. I decided to trust that the right time would come and was prepared to wait. This doesn't mean that it was an easy decision for me to terminate the pregnancy and it took me a while to get over the sadness of having lost yet another child.

My partner came to live with my Virgo girl and I in Australia and we began to create our lives together. We got married, his permanent residency in Australia was approved, I finished my studies and worked in various Government departments and my husband finally found secure full time job. Only then did we consider the possibility of having children together, after all with both of us having experience with separations and the heartbreak of him having to leave his daughter back in his country we were going to do our best to make sure we were settled to reduce the risk of history repeating itself.

My husband and I were discussing the possibility of trying for a baby when I received notice that my Father had passed away. This left a huge scar on my soul. My father was always my best friend and an inspiration to me, I adored my father so the grief that came over me was so much so that the thought of becoming pregnant at that time was too much to handle and we were going to put it on hold yet again, but it was too late.

I found out that I was pregnant with my second child only weeks after my father had passed. It was a bitter sweet experience. By this time my eldest child was already ten years old and I had to come to the acceptance that my father will never meet the rest of his grandchildren.

I fell back into depression triggered by the loss of my father at the same time as being pregnant. This brought up all sorts of emotional ups and downs. I felt constant anxiety within the pregnancy. I would be at home quietly putting clothes away and I'd suddenly start feeling heart palpitations and a feeling of panic like the ceilings were falling and the walls caving in on me. There were stages I thought I was going to have a heart attack. I tried to find every little remedy I could find like relaxation teas or the herbal drops under the tongue, meditation, I was willing to try anything natural.

Apparently my Mother survived her pregnancy with me taking Valium 3 times a day but I was determined that I wasn't going to go down the medical route again. I just remained as present as possible taking deep breaths till the feeling would pass by, and was grateful when it did.

As the pregnancy progressed the pressure of my husband needing to constantly go to Portugal to visit family and his daughter created lots of disharmony within our relationship. We decided to go together to Portugal to visit family before the baby was due not knowing when we would get another opportunity to travel after having more kids. There were continuous quarrels between my husband and I, I put it down to financial and responsibility stresses not for a lack of love, and we separated a few weeks before the birth of my second child, so after having my second baby girl, my Scorpio, PND take two kicked in full force.

My background and training gave me leverage this time. I knew exactly where to go for help and what to do to cope with my PND. I began to get Counselling sessions and worked on my childhood issues.

Luckily with the amount of training in child caring I now had, I could honestly say that I was happy with the way I parented my second child. Despite my depression I was present and involved, I was able to pick up my babies signs and baby cues quickly, interpret and attend to them quickly and as a result my Scorpio was a very happy, content and calm baby. Routines were on point and Mum life was predictable and smooth. My confidence in my parenting helped draw my Husband and I back together again, and my Scorpio child thrived.

My parenting experience with my Scorpio child was the perfect example of how parenting challenges can be overcome despite depression. If you get some experience with child caring, remain very present and aware with your child, not doing too many things at once and making the most of one-on-one time as well as having a good support system in place, parenting can be quite a joyful experience.

My Virgo was able to see an example of good parenting as my confidence radiated onto her also. I was feeling more successful as a mother, which was a huge priority to me after what I had gone through with my first child. My relationship with my Husband began to also improve immensely. This rollercoaster of a journey wasn't over yet. As our family settled we thought about not waiting too long before the next child.

We had the joy and pleasure of planning for baby number three. Let me tell you that there is a big difference between unplanned / surprise pregnancies and actually sitting down to discuss ovulation times, organizing that special evening and making love with the "intention" of creating a life. It's just such a beautiful, intense experience!

Most exciting, to do the pregnancy test together and see the results on the test "together". To know that discovering the news together was going to be a joyful welcomed experience. That fantasy of having your partner react like Tom Cruise in Cocktail where he picks her up in delight and announces to the world he's going to be a father is a dream come true at this point …. Well …. that's not exactly how it happened but was joyful none the less! Hey a Woman can dream can't she lol, but what actually happened next WAS unexpected…

CHAPTER NINE

Having children step children

I've decided to address the topic of step parenting as this was a challenge both my partner and I had to face. In this chapter I will mention some of the challenges my husband faced being a step Father and some of the challenges I faced being a step Mother.

Let's start with the issues around being a step Father. The role of step father is a role most Men aren't' prepared for. In our case it was lucky that my partner had a little girl around the same age as my little girl when we met so in essence he was already prepared for parenting a little girl but not for parenting someone else's little girl.

As a step Father you never know what role you are supposed to play in a child's life. In most cases step fathers want to be a more involved member of the family but they can soon find the biological connection of the mother and child will take sides against him and sometimes make him feel like an outsider looking into his own family. Feeling like they have no rights to be able to set rules and discipline the child in a way they would like.

In many step parenting cases the step child often expresses to the step parent "You are not my father" and so leaving the step parent often not only feeling left out but can often feel powerless and disrespected in his own home. The result of this leads to the parent feeling separated from the family and unappreciated for his role and efforts within the family. This was particularly relevant in our case. My partner's daughter lived overseas so the time my husband spent with his biological daughter was very limited, making my him feel guilty and resentful. It was unfair that he couldn't spent time with the daughter whom he wanted to spend time with. The step daughter he was raising didn't even appreciate his role within the family and what he was doing for her.

The dynamic in this type of household can be one of division so it's very important to make all family members feel as though they belong.

My particular issue around being a step mother was one of provincial value. In my mind my home was my territory and my nest. I was the Woman of my house and everyone else where children under my care. There was a hierarchy, my husband and I as the King and Queen and the children were people we needed to care for.

I always believed that children should be respectful of the adult's space and things. My children would have to ask before going into the cupboards to get something to eat, ask to come into my room and get things out of my drawers or ask if they were wanting to use something of mine.

Having another child coming into my home and not respecting my personal space or things was challenging for me. I felt like a hen looking after her nest and I didn't want to make space for any other hens, I felt like my step daughter was another hen trying to take over my nest or replace me. I realise this was a very primitive way of looking at things simply because I should be adult enough to set rules and reinforce them within my home, but my husband and I needed to be on the same page for this to occur.

When my step daughter would visit, my husband would switch to "Disneyland parenting" This is often a term used for parents who feel guilty about everything they couldn't do while the child was away so they give all they can within that little period of time that they have with the children. This would present an issue because the other children involved would feel like it was unfair treatment. Why weren't the rules the same for all of them and why was the visiting family member getting away with things the other kids weren't allowed to get away with. Often my daughter and I would feel pushed aside because the visiting daughter would take priority above everyone else in the family.

Another challenge in this situation is that my husband's ex-wife still played a big role in influencing our lives simply because she had control over the movements of my step daughter. So, we were always dependant what her decisions were around his daughter. My husband was always concerned about the welfare and whereabouts of his daughter every time his ex-wife would relocate to other countries for work purposes. It was sometimes hard to make long term family decisions because my husband often had to travel to visit his daughter overseas.

My step daughter is a very intelligent girl and very mature for her age. For this reason, I felt like she could manipulate situations and she knew how to press my buttons. These behaviours were no novelty to me as I was once a child from separated parents and I knew the game. Plus, my own Virgo daughter would occasionally play the same games between my husband and I. I admit it's sometimes harder to overlook these qualities when it's not your child who's playing the game and I was less forgiving of my step daughter's actions than my own daughter's actions.

After having children with my husband I noticed my energy begin to shift towards my children and what they needed became higher priority to me. My husband and I had shared goals. Now I'm not suggesting that people have children with their partner to fix a broken family dynamic. I'm simply acknowledging the fact that it put us both on the same page with regards to family goals, but then in essence both my husband and I have always valued family above everything else. Whereas in a dynamic where a couple may have conflicting goals, having more children could have placed more strain on a relationship and caused more reason for division within the relationship.

As my focus on what was good for the family grew I began to see and feel how hard it was for my husband to be away from his daughter and how much happier he was when his daughter was around. I would often ask myself the question...If I love and accept my husband then I should accept his daughter as a part of him and thus a part of me and our family. So if I want to see my husband happy I should love that piece of him within her, treat her as my own, encourage him to spend more time with her and do whatever I can to have her with us to complete the family. So, my view towards my step daughter began to shift and my role and duties as a step mother began to shift.

My step daughter moved in with us permanently when she was fourteen years old. Parenting teenagers is already challenging as it is without adding the extra fact that this teenager is technically not my child and she doesn't have to love or listen to me if she doesn't want to.

Having two teens around the same age helped them both settle. Both at home and at school. They were both in the same year and going through the same phases in life. This made the adjustment period slightly easier.

The younger kids at this point we're very excited to have another big sister around. My step daughter not having her biological mother around helped me to step more into a supportive role for her. There were occasions where I sympathised with my husband's feelings about earlier not feeling appreciated by my daughter and I was occasionally also feeling unappreciated for the role I had to now play towards another teenager.

There were ups and downs and moody emotional moments to be expected in a house full of Women but ultimately we were finally a complete family!

With puberty emotions and hormones become more of an issue. We were four women fighting for one Man's attention. My husband was put in a difficult position as he was trying to please all the women in his life without upsetting the other ones. As you can imagine this would be particularly hard around menstruation time as we were all synchronised and would all PMS around the same time. My husband didn't really have anywhere to escape to when we were all feeling very moody his only escape was occasional Soccer training.

Eventually tension did begin to rise. Were 6 people living in a 3 bedroom 1 bathroom home fighting for our own space. I discussed teenager issues with my doctor and I was comforted to find out that what I was going through was quite common. My doctor mentioned of the very high statistics of failed marriages due to the involvement of step children, in particular the involvement of "Daddy's Little Girl". He mentioned that Teenage girls and their connection with Daddy where the biggest culprits of most 2 time marriages failing.

My biggest challenge was learning to step back and allow my husband the space to be with his daughter. I wanted my husband to function as the one who kept the whole family on common ground and united but when my step daughter lived with us permanently her neediness was very apparent and I noticed all of the focus going towards her needs.

In my mind my step daughter needed a Father more than I needed a Husband so I began to step back to allow for that to happen. As you can imagine disconnecting from my Husband and step daughter created even more inner turmoil for me. I began to feel lack of control over my home and the emotional distance from my partner that I became more controlling and possessive over everything in my household that was mine. My insecurities made me look at my step daughter like the other Woman who came into my home and stole my life.

The truth was my step daughter had gone through some big challenges already from such a young age that forced her to become very insecure and controlling herself. She was just doing what she thought she needed to do to survive. At the end of the day she was a good kid and in all honesty, she was just confronting me with myself as a teenager, forcing me to look at my unresolved demons.

I noticed that on occasions I would stay quiet to keep the peace. I learnt to pick my battles and my silence became my strength. Unfortunately, my silence in most battles made my Virgo daughter feel unsafe and unprotected. My Virgo began to see me as someone weak who couldn't stand up for myself or for her for that matter. Ultimately I had to learn to respect myself and my child enough to set these boundaries, which can be very hard when you are trying to please everyone in your life. You want your child to feel safe and cared for but at the same time you also want your partner to feel appreciated and involved.

My internal lesson within my step parenting experience was learning to set personal boundaries. I had to become clear about my boundaries with my step daughter and my step daughter's boundaries in relation to me and my husband. I also had to voice what my partner had a right to say to my child and what I wouldn't tolerate in relation to both the teens.

My experience around step parenting encouraged me to call my step mother and apologise for everything I put her through as a teenager. My step mother always seemed very distant and cold to me, but after being a step mother myself I realise it was just a defence or self-protective mechanism to avoid me taking advantage of her. I obviously didn't appreciate or see all that she did for me at the time, but 25 years later, I now appreciate all that she did for me and the role that she played in my life. My step mother proceeded to give me the most valuable advice I could ever give towards another family dealing with step parenting. She said "Carla the most important thing is that you remain the mature adult in this situation and that you and your husband communicate and stick together in your decisions."

So here is my best piece of advice if you're considering having children when step children are already involved. Children need to see that both parents are committed and on the same page over rules, discipline, morals and goals within the family. They need to see that there is no division between mother and father regardless of biological or step parenting roles. The household needs to function harmoniously as a family unit and the mother and father are at the head of that family unit. Family is a team, and a great team needs confident and connected leaders. Make decisions together and don't let children play you against each other. It is your job as adults to set the example.

Slightly off topic I can say one great thing my parents taught me. Even though both my parents were separated and re-married they always kept their relationship amicable for my sake. Furthermore, I was probably one of the rare children at a young age that could have Christmas dinners, Easter, Birthdays or just about any special occasions with all of my family together, My Mum, Step Dad, Dad and Step Mum all at the same time. There was no animosity that I felt between anyone at any time or it there was they always kept it all very mature and very well hidden. I tried my best to carry this forward between my daughter's father and I for the sake of my daughter. And I always tried to stay amicable with my husband's ex-wife for my step-daughter's her sake also.

CHAPTER TEN

The planned unexpected

Feeling slightly more confident within my parenting after my second baby girl came along I was very excited and optimistic when I got pregnant again a year or so after my Scorpio. Sadly, I had a miscarriage. We decided to try again six months later.

I finally became pregnant again. During this pregnancy I had bleeding and cramps at eleven weeks gestation. Feeling scared that a miscarriage was happening all over again my husband and I went for an emergency ultrasound only to find out that while I did in fact miscarry a baby there was still another baby very much alive and well. I didn't even know this was possible. So my baby number three is a twin. I counted my blessings and did my best to try and take it easy hoping not to lose my other baby. Taking it easy was not in my cards. The next day my husband ended up in hospital only to have his gallbladder removed, I continued to work on my Spray Tanning business which I opened to get some extra income on the weekends and look after the other two children.

At my first trimester screening and testing for Down's Syndrome they categorised me as a very high risk for the possibility of Down's Syndrome so my doctor sent me to do an Amniocentesis. I tell you this was one of the most frightening things I've had to do. The procedure in itself was uncomfortable and I was scared of the risk to my baby. But what frightened me the most was what would possibly happen afterwards. What if my child had Down's Syndrome? what decision would I make, if I had enough time to make a decision at all? It was a torturous 3 weeks waiting for the results. Luckily they all came back negative to DS and we had a couple of months of smooth sailing.

At around 7 months the midwives found out I had Polyhydramnios (Excess of Amniotic Fluid) which presented a few risks and concerns. I was having ultrasounds fortnightly then weekly till the birth. Towards the end I knew in my heart something didn't feel right. After this many pregnancies I knew my body well. I noticed that my body would threaten to go into labour and I would feel the baby drop and contractions then suddenly I'd feel the baby start vigorously kicking and shaking, she would disengage, move back up and the contractions would stop. It was unlike anything I had ever felt with my previous pregnancies. My senses were telling me this baby is too scared to be born.

At every Ultrasound I asked the sonographer to check her neck for the Umbilical cord as this was one of the risks of having Polyhydramnios. More importantly it was my instinct telling me this was what was going on and being an intuitive I needed to trust my gut warnings. They kept reassuring me there was nothing around her neck but admitted that if it was around her neck that it would be hard to tell from an Ultrasound.

When I eventually went into labour I was fully dilated and ready to push within two and a half hours. She came out very blue in the face and sure enough she had the cord wrapped around her neck twice. What was happening was the more I pushed the tighter it got around her neck because the placenta was at the top of my uterus. I believe my deceased father and all my Angels were watching over us that day. The nurse quickly untangled her, gave her a rub to encourage her breathing and placed her in my arms. When I finally saw her breathing and get some colour back on her little face the relief on both my husband's and my face was evident, and so began the journey with my very extra sensory child, my Aries.

Having the responsibility of a teen, a two-year-old, working, running a business and now a new born presented some extra challenges for me. Having a new born that didn't sleep between 12am till 4am created serious exhaustion. The moment I'd put my new born down or walk out of the room she would scream. My Aries would never sleep longer than 20- 30mins at a time. I felt some symptoms of PND within the few weeks and I didn't waste a moment. I went back to my counsellor and she helped me join a PND mothers group which turned out to be the best thing I ever did. Having that support was GODSEND. I continued to breastfeed as this seemed to be the only thing that could soothe my baby and me at the time. With such a busy schedule, breastfeeding would maintain that small time out for bonding with my baby.

The challenge I didn't consider at the time was the closeness in age. Bonding with one without neglecting the others was tough. Time management was a must. I had to make sure I could give my time equally to both the younger ones who still very much needed me. Sadly, my teen would often fall into the background and feel unnoticed. So I had to pay particular attention to the fact that she was feeling left out and try make one on one time with her when I could.

My Aries was very demanding she would tantrum immediately if she didn't get what she wanted within seconds of expressing her needs, as I mentioned she was a bad sleeper and eventually diagnosed with a sleeping disorder. She was an extra sensory child. If she fell asleep with a specific background noise I couldn't change the background noise without waking her, she'd get over stimulated easily and go hyper, she would wake up if she felt a pressure change in the room or someone walk in, she was extremely scared of the dark, if there was a loud noise she would jump in fright or put her hands over her ears, she was terrified to get dressed and couldn't have shirts go over her head without going into a panic and almost hyperventilate if the shirt took too long to come down over her face. She would panic to the point of where her legs would start shaking and sometimes she would actually have to sit down for me to dress her. I'm convinced this was a trauma carried from labour and her experience with the umbilical cord. She was awake every night at the exact times. There were nights I would get angry and scream at her out of pure frustration and nights I ended up crying myself to sleep beside her bed while holding her hand. I prayed for God to give me enough strength not to hurt her.

I felt so emotionally drained constantly. Only now do I realise how important that bonding process was for us. I'm so glad I continued to breastfeed till 9 months. I truly believe that because I had created a good bond with her from the beginning through the breastfeeding I was able to tolerate much more than I had tolerated from all my other children. Even though she was the hardest child thus far I was able to step back and look at her with love and compassion. But then I don't know if this was due to maturity also. I was able to step back and become the observer of my temper and realise that she's only being a child, learning, pushing boundaries and I will love her no matter how much she was exhausting me.

In conclusion I wasn't consumed by the PND to the point of where I wasn't able to function. Even though I had every reason to fall back into a serious depression. I realised this time one thing was different. Not only the confidence within myself as a mother but the compassion towards myself as a human. When I felt down I seeked help. When I wasn't coping I'd ask for support from those around me. When I needed time for myself even if it was just to take 5 mins for a cup of tea I did it. Being a mother is not only about nurturing someone else it's about the mother nurturing herself enough to be able to offer that nurturing to another human being. As a result of this self-love as a mother I was abler to teach my children how they should treat themselves and expect to be treated by others.

CHAPTER ELEVEN

Parenting today

After years of being a parent I was starting to think that I really didn't like parenting. Really, what I disliked is society's concept of what parenting should look like! Society creates an expectation that makes it so parents are made to feel bad for whatever they do. If you can't keep your child quiet in a supermarket you are a bad parent. If your child is throwing a tantrum, it's because you're an out of control parent and don't discipline properly. If your child is sad and unfriendly it's because you're not present for your child and have abandoned them when they've needed you most. If you're a working Mum, then your honoured as a contributor to society but if you're a stay at home mum nurturing your children then you aren't contributing to society and so on. In essence nothing you ever do is right.

Psychologists will continue to conduct studies that will forever contradict other studies, and new theories will continue to be born. so how will we ever know what is the best way to parent our children. Parenting 50 years ago was completely different to parenting ten years ago. I find that within my parenting experience alone I have a ten-year age gap between my first two children. In that ten-year age gap we as a society went from teaching parents that children should be left to cry and self soothe to staying in the room with them, carrying the child as much as possible and co-sleeping. I went from being taught that a child should be on routines to now attending to our children when they need and allowing them to follow and trust their own biological clock when it comes to routines. Just within my parenting experience it went from parent led parenting to child led parenting.

I propose a new way of looking at parenting, I propose the idea of not really Parenting as such. I propose taking on the role of the Co-creator! A Co-creator means someone who creates something jointly with another person or people. In essence we are all creators. As a parent we are a creator who gave physical life to another creator. A parent's job is to nurture a child's individual gifts and talents in order for them to become a happy human that is able to align easily towards their own creation, so in essence a parent is a co-creator.

As much as most humans would like to think that they are independent and don't need anyone, we live in a co-dependent universe where we all need each other and each person plays an important role on this planet. We need the postman just as much as we need the garbage man just as much as we need the doctors and nurses. We are all Creators. Our job as a Co-creator is to help our children become the best creators of their own world that they can be and aid the expansion of this universe.

I've come to the conclusion that there is no such thing as the perfect parent. If there is a perfect parent out there, please show me and tell me why you have come to this conclusion? If there was a perfect parent out there we would assume that their child would never have experienced the contrast of what a bad parent is. If there was a perfect parent out there, then what would these perfect children look like and would they all turn out exactly the same as each other. Furthermore, how would that serve towards the expansion of consciousness having billions of exactly the same like-minded people running around all doing the exact same thing.

The concept of a Co-creator is an idea that can be applied to all aspects of parenting. Children are just as much creators of this universe as we are. In pure electro-magnetic form, they are no lower or higher than adults. As pure energy beings they are equal. Just because they came here in smaller and more fragile body doesn't mean their spirit is weak or that they are any less deserving, are any less human, any less special or have any less potential than us.

Taking away the Hierarchy of "I am parent, you are just child" brings about a relationship based on compassion, mutual understanding and equality. The battle for power is no longer a necessary one as a Co- creator parent understands that the nurturing and compassion they instil in a child is not for the purpose of self- indulgence, self-validation or self-significance, it's simply a gift from one Human to another.

The role of a Co-creator parent is to keep a child safe and healthy long enough for them to eventually step out into their own Creator role. Being the Co-creator doesn't mean that you are responsible for your child's creations, it simply means that you have nurtured and supported an open minded child that feels safe and free enough to express and mould themselves into whatever they choose to become. Ultimately the Co- creator parent understands that they are simply a first step in the child's life. The Co-creator parent lays good foundations for the child based on the child's individual needs and desires. It's not the Co-creator's responsibility of what their children become but it is the Co-creator's responsibility to provide the necessary ingredients for creation to freely take place. I chose to home-school my children for this reason. I wanted to help nurture their individual gifts and skills.

I wish we had a course as a part of the early childhood study programs in high schools to introduce the concept of the role of a Co-Creator Parent. I wish teenagers especially understood how much of an important role they play in their children's lives and how they affect their children through their actions and behaviours. Having teenage Girls, myself I'm faced on a daily basis with the careless remarks they make around getting pregnant and having children, like it's just the flavour of the week! Having a child is not like having a Dog or changing your clothes. It's a life time decision. If only everyone would learn about parenting and the need for emotional stability within the self before considering having children and taking on the role of a Co-creator. In this course I would introduce the idea of Shadow work and Inner child healing to teach people how to become stable enough within their own emotions to be able to help create good foundations for others.

One day my teenage daughter was talking about pregnancy and having children like it was no big deal just something people do when they feel like it. So I said to her, "Go look in the mirror and tell yourself you love yourself and that you are beautiful just the way you are!" She couldn't do it and obviously refused seeing no point in my request. I proceeded to say. "If you can't even do that how do you expect to teach a child to be confident and love themselves?"

How much do you value you?? And what's values are you able to teach a child within and for themselves if you don't value you?

CHAPTER TWELVE

My childhood

I come from an interesting family of hot blooded Portuguese. My mother was a compliant, shy and a non-confrontational Woman who focused mostly on trying to be the perfect wife. She created her identity around how well she could cook, clean, wash and do everything around the house, learning to balance all of this plus working full time and taking care of my brother or I where possible. Her childhood was extremely traumatic. Due to My Grandmother's depression my Mum was raised in the city by her very wealthy Godmother being very spoiled. Sadly, this didn't last as she was to be ripped away from everything she knew at the age of 9 and put back with her biological family (along with her other 3 sisters) whom she had never met. She remembers saying to her biological Mother 'You're not my real Mum you people took me away from my real Mum' (In Portuguese of course) and her biological father was very abusive so she suffered with constant nervousness, anxiety and depression herself. She couldn't see the opportunity to get married and move away from home fast enough and married her first boyfriend to whom she got pregnant to at the age of 19 who is today a VERY famous actor in Portugal. She had my eldest brother whom is 11 years older than I.

My father was a poor country boy living with both parents and another Brother and Sister, working from a very young age and only getting his first pair of shoes at the age of 9. However, his family life seemed to be slightly more stable. He also married young and had a Son to his first wife who is my second eldest brother being 10 years older than I. Anyways this was just to give you a brief idea of my parent's background. My parents were 2 very different people.

My Dad was interesting in the sense that it's like he always had 2 people inside him. He was very caring and protective of his immediate family and incredible with children (Children were drawn to him, he always looked like Santa Clause with his beard and sparkling brown eyes always ready to joke around) yet he had a dark side. Even though he was caring towards me he drank far too much and was very emotionally and physically abusive towards my mother.

I have scary but very vague memories of abuse towards my Mother. I remember once my father helping my mother put her clothes on and I saw her arms covered in bruises. At the time I didn't understand it I would have been around four or five years old but as an adult I began to put all the scenes in my memory together and make sense of things.

Every time I asked my parents to clarify some of my childhood events none of their stories seemed to match up. Interestingly, I was very intuitive and was able to recollect some things that had happened. There were lots of missing pieces but there were also bits where I could remember things that happened with precise accuracy from the age of 6 months onwards. So as much as they wanted to hide most of what was going on between them I felt everything.

My father walked out on my mother and I shortly after we all moved from Portugal to Australia. My mother not knowing much English, not having work or family to support her was left in a difficult situation of survival to raise a child in a foreign country. When my father tried to come back into our lives almost 1 year later feeling very remorseful over what he had done my mum had already met what was to become my first step Father.

At this stage I still rarely saw my Dad, but when I did I would often ask my dad if I could stay with him. One day my Dad decided to grant my wish and tried to keep me longer which resulted in my mum coming with the police to pick me up. This was a very scary experience for a 6-year-old. My father lived in an apartment at the time and the Police asked via loud speaker to come downstairs. As I detached from my dad and walked over to the police and my mum I remember turning around and seeing my dad with his hands up in the air and the police walking his direction. It's all a bit of a blur from that point and I didn't see my dad for a while after that.

My father had a few girlfriends after my Mum but he soon settled with a wonderful lady who became my first Step Mum. Being very possessive of my Dad I would fight with often but later grew to adore and admire her tremendously.

A lot happened to me between the ages of 5-7 years' old that were enough to turn me into a very scared insecure child. Simply writing about these brief moments in my childhood causes anxiety within me. Moving from my homeland at the age of 5yo I never felt at home anywhere. I had this constant nagging feeling that I just wasn't from here. In reality I never felt home anywhere, only in my mind.

It was particularly hard being in a strange country being put in to primary school without knowing the language. I was constantly bullied and made fun of because I didn't understand the other kids and looked different. I wasn't popular because I didn't have blonde hair and blue eyes like the popular kids in Bondi. I was seen as the WOG kid. When I was in kindergarten the kids in year 6 would sit me on their lap pretending to befriend me then 2 or 3 kids would hold me down as the others would pull the hairs on my legs. My mother would never let me shave my legs so even when I changed primary schools the nickname Magilla gorilla seemed to always stick. My mother had strong views around shaving, believing that I would become hairier if I shaved so she wouldn't let me. To top it off she cut my hair short and I looked like a boy with these HUGE thick magnifying type of glasses on my face.

I think parents sometimes don't realise the damage their choices and actions have on their children. No matter how trivial those decisions seem to them. Or maybe they do, but choose to ignore it thinking that it will pass because they're just children and parents think children are too young to understand or remember it all. Never really offering much by way of support or guidance through big transitions in life. Financially we were the average family so I can't say I ever had any worries around finances, Health wise I was always a pretty healthy child but emotionally I was a mess.

Moving forward, life was challenging for me. I had to adjust to the new man in my mother's life not because I was jealous simply because my gut feeling always told me not to trust him. Something always felt shady about him and every time I'd try to tell my mother how I felt about my step father she would devalue what I said responding with "Don't be silly, he loves you!".

Once I had a nightmare that felt so real I could step into it. The nightmare was of my step father all bandaged up in the hospital and he grabbed my mum and hid her under his hospital bed because his lover had walked in the room. This dream was a premonition, only months later my mother found out my step dad was cheating on her and she retaliated by striking him with a rolling pin constantly as he was trying to sleep. He was very bruised, and I was the one that had to stop the fight getting in between him and my mother. That must be why he was bandaged in my dream. I had just turned 15 years old at the time. My intuition was right!

I was often put in situations where I was made to feel emotionally responsible my Mother. My relationship with my mother was very strained. I never felt like I could succeed in her eyes. She was very emotionally vulnerable and unstable and I often felt like I was walking on egg shells. Too scared my actions would cause her a nervous breakdown but at the same time crying out for some attention.

When my Mum finally divorced my step father I was 16 years old. My mum fell into a deep depression and I became the ping pong ball passed from person to person till she was able to get back on her feet. At an age when I felt I needed a stable figure the most I really had no one solid to lean on or guide me, everyone was too busy with their own lives. My mother often threatened to take a full box of pills and take her life. I never knew whether I was one day going to find her dead which created extra anxiety. At 16 I couldn't cope with her emotions and mine too I knew she needed me but I just didn't yet know how to be there for myself much less for her.

I found that due to my lack of connection with my Mother I was forever needing Mother like figures. I always felt this constant need to seek approval from older wiser Women. This was my "Mummy" issues constantly resurfacing, that childhood aspect of me begging to be healed. Until I eventually learned to love and accept myself the way I was, good and bad aspects, this was a huge issue for me because I found it hard to connect to other females as I didn't trust them. Once I resolved to no longer care what other Women thought of me, I stopped seeking approval and I began to make more honest relationships with Women.

My Father began to play more of a role in my life when I moved to Perth. I would have been nearly 10 years old at the time. As a teen He and my Step Mother became my best friends and my go to people for advice and rescuing.

I began working with him when I was 16 years old at his restaurant.

My Father was the optimistic parent who made me believe that I could do anything that I put my mind to. He was a Chef so he loved his food and wine, in fact he was the one who taught me how to cook. Often drinking more than he should, He was a lady's man and my step mother did have her challenges with him, but they were so good at communicating they seemed to overcome most challenges. I caused so many fights between my Dad and Step-Mum just being typical Daddy's girl, but my Step-Mum was incredibly patient and brutally honest with me in a mature way. I appreciated that. She was an emotionally stable Woman so I felt safe with her. I always knew I could be my cheeky self around her without her losing her temper or having a nervous breakdown and I could ask her anything as she was very open minded about EVERYTHING!

Falling into relationship after relationship seeking love and approval from guys. I got engaged at the age of seventeen. I left high school and felt as though my only purpose for living would be to have a family of my own. I saw children as something that would be mine and would never leave me. I was in such a hurry to grow up and have children of my own without any real example of what great parenting looked like. It's like I was just searching for the perfect relationship constantly to have children with I never once considered whether my boyfriends would be a good father, a good support or lifelong partner, it was just hormonal and instinctual I wanted kids and no one was going to stop me! Such an immature childish way of thinking!

I continued in this mindset, got engaged at the tender age of 17 (Which lasted only 1 year) and after breaking up with my fiancé started dating in the search for the perfect husband again. Looking for the perfect husband would entail me actually knowing what the perfect Husband was, but since I never had much of an example of what this looked like I was searching blindly. I constantly felt like both an old soul (with an awareness of a bigger power in the world) and an immature child (not having yet developed proper emotional intelligence) trapped in a human body. I definitely wasn't ready to be any kind of example for another Human Child.

CHAPTER THIRTEEN

The role of the Co-creator?

Let's start from the beginning. Babies are born with no sense of self or separation from others or the world. They are born with a sense of connection and oneness to everything that exists. What they can see with their eyes is images that all bleed into one image, there's no definition or clarity yet, no sense of where they start and you begin. Which is why when someone sneezes around a baby they don't understand that it wasn't them that made the sneezing noise, when someone jumps they get a fright or when someone who's holding them feels anxiety or sadness they also feel unsettled, anxious or sad.

As babies grow they begin to learn that they are separate. There becomes a more defined separate between them and the World around them. As they become socialised they learn that certain emotions, feelings and actions aren't acceptable. They are taught to suppress, repress, deny, ignore, control or mask these unacceptable emotions, feelings and actions. If they don't control their emotions, feelings and actions they will be shamed, punished or abandoned for expressing themselves. Essentially they learn that to be them self is not OK. For example - When a child falls down and is feeling sad or hurt because over the fall then the parent says to the child "you're ok! Up you get!" This teaches the child that there's something wrong with what they are feeling because the child does NOT feel ok but the parent is telling them that they are OK. Furthermore, saying that there is nothing wrong, therefore causing the child to stop trusting their own feelings and perception of what happened. As a result, the child feels like they can't trust their own emotional internal guidance system, basically can't trust themselves to know what does and doesn't feel good for them.

The child will then base their thoughts and ideas of what is true and what is false on what their primary carer thinks is true or false. This gives rise to the Ego self to be formed as a survival instinct, but we'll look deeper into that in a moment.

First and foremost, to be a Co-Creator the parent needs to step into the idea that there is no Hierarchy amongst them and their children. Just because children come into the world in smaller bodies doesn't mean that they are any less or more than any other human or carry a weaker energy or spirit. They have the right to be alive, to eat and breathe the same as everyone else in the world. When a child is confronted with an adult standing over them, the child looks up feeling vulnerable and intimidated, like looking up at a giant. Try this as an exercise. Have yourself sit on the floor and ask another person to stand over you with a very authoritative attitude and yelling at you? It can be quite scary and intimidating for a child. When an adult has the mentality that a child is less than them and becomes angry towards a small child all the child perceives is the rush of angry energy coming towards him/her. The child stops listening to the words and simply tries to interpret the gust of overpowering anger rushing at them. Putting them into a powerless and wordless fearful state. No one can make good decisions from that state of fear and powerlessness.

Usually by the age of 2 or 3 years old a child begins to try and express their independence and individuality. What they call the terrible 2's is often when the primary Carer begins to realise that their child now is a separate person to them, the Carer realises they have little power over the child's individual wants, expressions, desires and interests. Children begin to show signs of their individual skills and talents. When the child shows interest in creating their own path in life, primary carers can feel discarded by their child feeling like they're no longer wanted or needed by the child. This is where the parent can lose their temper quicker and things that used to be acceptable when the child was a baby is no longer acceptable. This confuses the child making their Ego step in with full force survival mode.

The Ego is an entity created in the mind after having been hurt, shamed or rejected that feels the need to step in to ensure your physical survival by taking over control. It doesn't like to feel powerless. The wounded Ego can be perceived as selfish simply because it's whole energy goes into ensuring your survival sometimes disregarding needs or feelings of others. It will do everything it can to justify its fears and preserve its power. However, the Ego is not all bad, having a healthy Ego is actually necessary for human physical survival. It provides the opportunity for people to differentiate between what's right from wrong for for them. It can help people distinguish themselves from others. It encourages people to explore their individual talents and unique gifts. It helps people assert themselves, strive for growth, draw boundaries, safeguard and protect themselves. In a healthy state the Ego loves life which is why it appoints itself as the Governor of your physical world.

When the primary Carer's Ego becomes more attached to what their expectations of the child is. In today's society parents and primary carers are very attached to whether their child will be a doctor or a lawyer and bring honour or shame to their family. There are many parent's trying to live their own personal lives or losses through their own children. When parent's become this attached to their child's decisions the Co-creator role takes on a very controlling role.

As a Co-creator, your job is to acknowledge and nurture the child's natural gifts and talents. Remember that the child came through you but does not belong to you. This is a concept that is very hard for parents to grasp. You can never own another human being and forcing them to become what you want them to become is taking away their freedom to be their own expression of themselves. It can be challenging for the parent when a child shows interests in things that are outside of the parent's norm of interests. Parents can become influencing or judgmental around the interests of the child. Ideally the Co-creator would not make the child feel wrong or ashamed for what they are interested in.

The Co-creator should trust that the child knows what feels right for them. The Co-creator should encourage self-directed learning and it's my personal belief and opinion that the direction of the education system should be headed this way! If your child interested in Dinosaurs allow and encourage them to explore the world of Dinosaurs as much as possible, till they either lose interest of move onto their next interest. If a child is taught from a young age to enjoy exploring their own interests, you will find that they very naturally gravitate towards their preferred career path quite early on in life. As one door closes another door opens and then leads to another without any resistance or forcing. The child is then free to find where they fit into the world and as a result find their role in society sooner.

As long as the Co-creator is there for their child and nurturing their desires and interests by teaching them to be true to themselves and helping them become creators of their own world, the Co-creator is building a happy confident child. A happy confident child is less likely to become a problem to society. Happy people don't usually feel the need to go out and disturb other people's lives or create disharmony in their community. They're usually an asset to the world as the world can always benefit from having happy internally fulfilled people. As a result, these children will make a Co- creator feel as though they've done a good parenting job within any great strain to parent. The Co-creator will enjoy being able to have taken part of the nurturing of this child's own creations without needing to own any responsibility for their child's individual choices.

Creating this type of compassionate relationship with child will create a happier more connected relationship between Parent and Child. These children will appreciate and understand the connectedness of everything and all humans. You can't separate the artist from the art, the Art carries the artist's energy and influence. You are a Creator adore your creation, your children are your creations, as they are an expression of you, becoming Creators of their own World!

The Co-Creator in action

The concept of Unconditional love. Being a parent is the closest thing you will get to knowing what unconditional love is. Rather than looking at it as unconditional love I'm going to call it acceptance. When a baby is born a parent naturally accepts all aspects of the child. A parent accepts how the baby looks, accepts the fact that the baby is going to soil their nappies, accepts that it's going to cry, accepts that it's going to need to be fed and need to be taken care of.

However, at some point where the child is not complying with the parent's expectations there is a shift. Maybe the child is not sleeping or not listening to what the parent has asked of them and that acceptance turns into 'conditional love'. Conditional on the behaviour of the child. If the child is displaying behaviours that are in contradiction to what the parent expects or believes to be appropriate, the parent is no longer in acceptance of the child. E.g.: "I will only accept you based on the condition that you behave in a way which is appropriate to what I need or expect of you" It's Important to remain conscious of every time you have an interaction with a child. Ask yourself "Am I reacting out of my attachment to my needs and expectations of what I want this child to do, or am I acting from a place of acceptance for this child's individuality independent of my expectations of them?" Stepping back in this way allows you to become the observer and can help you make decisions based more around compassion considering everyone's needs rather than attachment to your own outcome. Recognise when you're simply controlling or forcing a child to do something so that you can feel more comfortable as you are observing them. All you are trying to do is stop your own discomfort with watching them do something you don't like.

It's not just about taking care of physical needs of the child it's also the emotional needs of the child.

As a Co-Creator you're not only responsible for making sure the child is fed, kept warm and safe it's also important to acknowledge their emotional needs. In the first couple of years of a child's life they don't have the vocabulary to express themselves properly. Therefore, most of the communication involves crying and body language. (I highly recommend parents look into a Baby Body Language Course). Knowing baby body language can be valuable to avoid delay in the interpretation of a child's needs and behaviour. Avoiding this delay can save the child and parent a lot of frustration and anxiety.

When a baby is young and you believe that you have taken care of all their basic needs such as being fed, nappy changed and rugged them up warm but the baby is still crying, I would consider The Release method. This method involves you going somewhere quiet if possible with the baby, holding the baby close to you and allowing the baby to cry in your arms. Allow baby to feel safe and close to you and whisper in the baby's ear "I'm here for you!" If at any point you feel frustration or anxiety come up where you feel unable to cope with their release of emotions, see if someone else in a calm state can do it for you. The idea is to remain as present and calm as possible for your child so that they know that they're safe to express their emotions without feeling abandoned, judged or unaccepted. This method can also be helpful in toddlerhood. You will find that in the future the child will feel safe to come to whomever allowed them to express their feelings freely. They will seek out comfort in knowing that they will still be accepted by the person who allowed them to express themselves.

Practicing the release method will help the child feel as though it's Ok to have different emotions even the unpleasant ones. Emotions are a human's internal guidance system and will trigger a child's instinctual reactions. The last thing you want to do is make them feel as though their emotions are wrong and cause a child to switch this guidance system off. It's like turning off the Humanity Switch in 'Vampire Diaries' It will be detrimental to their survival in future out in society and could cause serious dysfunctional behaviours.

I still practice this with my children today. I've spent many times where I've had to stop what I was doing and sit on my kitchen floor to hug them, practice presence and allow my child to release their emotions. I knew when my child was ready to move on when they'd start taking deep breaths and were open to communication again after their release. You will notice children have the instinct to touch base or what they associate to home and safety occasionally, in most cases for young children the parent is the home base or safe zone. Once they've touched base and recharged for a while they usually then feel safe enough to go back out to have another adventure. You as the parent providing that safe zone for them whenever it's necessary gives them the security they need each time they are feeling insecure, unsure or unsafe. Kids who know that the parent (their safe zone) is available to them whenever they need generally are more willing to go out and explore the World as long as they can occasionally touch home base once in a while. Unfortunately, this does make the parent feel completely emotionally drained when the child is done, but let's leave that 'self-care' subject for another chapter.

Shadow work teaching children to work through their emotions, fears and anxieties. The keys to helping a child through an emotion is Presence and Acceptance. When you can see a child feeling overwhelming emotions that they don't understand and can't express sit down with the child and help them work through their feelings and emotions. The intention is not to fix their emotion. Trying to fix or remove the emotion would indicate that there is something wrong with it to begin with. It's simply allowing them an opportunity to reflect on the emotion and begin to pick up what triggers those emotions.

We all have positive aspects and negative aspects within our being, but both serve a purpose. Both good and bad together like Yin and Yang make us one whole. We work through our Shadow (hidden) negative aspects of self with the intention of validating and acknowledging the feeling. This gives the feeling space to be expressed and dissipate naturally on its own. These feelings are there for a purpose.

A feeling comes up or is triggered so that it can be healed. If a feeling is coming up repeatedly it's a warning that there is a certain aspect of self that has not been acknowledged or healed, so it will continue to come up until it's had the opportunity to be acknowledged, expressed and healed.

For example: If a child is upset because someone took their toy and has gone into an emotional tantrum calmly say to the child "How are you feeling?" Or if they are too young to understand you can suggest "It looks like you may be feeling angry about something?" Or you can show them feeling picture cards and ask them which one they think they are feeling. Allow the child to express what they can about what happened with presence and understanding. Validate and Explain to them that they have a right to feel upset and feel how they feel when someone took something off them. No one would like that! If they want to cry, scream, talk more or even be quiet let them know that you are there with them while they are working through those emotions.

When the child has expressed all they've wanted to express you'll notice a sudden shift in their body language. Their breathe becomes deeper and longer and you can see the tension in the muscles of their body and face begin to soften. In some cases, children can look very limp or tired and in some cases they may even fall asleep. When they have entered a more open state of mind then you can discuss with them alternative options around playing with the toy. As them if they can think of a possible solution to the problem, possibly getting a new toy. Allow them some moments of presence to come up with ideas on how to resolve the issue. This will hand power back over to them. The most important thing is that you've validated their feelings and emotions first without making them feel abandoned, rejected or ashamed for feeling what they have felt.

This is essential for the growing child's sense of trust in their own internal guidance system. A great story about being in acceptance of both your good and bad traits and not making them wrong is the old tale about the White

Wolf Black Wolf. The story goes like this. Grandfather says to his Grandson, "*A fight is going on inside me. It is a terrible fight and it is between two wolves. One is evil – he is full of anger, envy, sorrow, regret, greed, arrogance, self-pity, guilt, resentment, inferiority, lies, false pride, superiority, and ego. The other is good – he is full of joy, peace, love, hope, serenity, humility, kindness, benevolence, empathy, generosity, truth, compassion, and faith. The same fight is going on inside you – and inside every other person, too.*" Grandson asks, "*Which wolf will win?*" The Grandfather says, "*If you feed them right, they both win. You see, if I only choose to feed the white wolf, the black one will be hiding around every corner waiting for me to become distracted or weak and jump to get the attention he craves. He will always be angry and always fighting the white wolf. But if I acknowledge him, he is happy and the white wolf is happy and we all win. For the black wolf has many qualities tenacity, courage, fearlessness, strong-willed and great strategic thinking that I have need of at times and that the white wolf lacks. But the white wolf has compassion, caring, strength and the ability to recognise what is in the best interest of all. You see, son, the white wolf needs the black wolf at his side. To feed only one would starve the other and they will become uncontrollable. To feed and care for both means they will serve you well and do nothing that is not a part of something greater. Feed them both and there will be no more internal struggle for your attention. And when there is no battle inside, then there is peace and you can listen to the voices of deeper knowing that will guide you in choosing what is right in every circumstance."*

This story explains the benefits of each emotion be it good or bad. Both serve a purpose and both make a person complete whole.

Learning through the consequences of their actions.

Children learn best through the consequences of their actions. Safety is always first and foremost so I'm not saying to allow your child to cross the street on their own before they are noticeably ready. However, rescuing your child from every possible hazard doesn't do anything for their personal growth and it won't teach them to take responsibility for their actions as well as delay a lot of their developmental milestones. You can tell a child 10 times that a candle is hot but some children simply won't understand what hot means until they actually put their finger to the flame. It's better to allow a child to have a small burn if it means in the long run they will learn that fire is dangerous.

At every opportunity possible discuss with your child their choices and what the possible outcomes might be if they are old enough to understand. Where they aren't old enough then a small consequence is a small price to pay if it teaches them to take responsibility for their bigger choices with bigger consequences when they get older.

Violence doesn't solve anything.

Teaching children on a daily basis should be a humbling experience. The physical fragility of children's little bones and stature needs to be taken into consideration but is by no means an indication of a weakness of Spirit. We live in a society that believes in reward and punishment. Hopefully we will continue to move towards a new more compassionate way of teaching children. We can't punish someone into happiness, we can't smack someone into goodness and we can't devalue someone's feelings in the hope they'll become compassionate towards others.

We often don't realise the consequences of our parenting decisions or see the correlation between what we do to our children and how they turn out. It's time to take responsibility for our parenting actions! Having power battles with children hoping that Wars over power don't happen is a contradiction! As Gandhi said "An eye for an eye leaves the whole world blind!" Holding Anger towards another human is like drinking the poison yourself in the hope that the other person will die. Many times do you see people being extra polite and nice to other people's children but when they go home they are impatient, rude and aggressive towards their own children. Be kind to your children. Compassion starts at home be careful what and how you teach them to resolve their problems.

Law of attraction.

Feelings and thoughts emit a frequency. As Humans we are made up of an Electro-magnetic field. Thoughts create electrical waves and Emotions create magnetic waves. Both Thoughts and feelings together create this electromagnetic field and it's a harmonious synchronicity of Heart and Mind.

Teach your children about the Law of attraction. Show them by example how to attract what they want into their life. If a child shows feels and thinks compassionate towards another Child, they will attract compassion back. If a child shows anger and aggression towards another Child, they will only be met with more anger and aggression. A child who feels in the constant victim lonely mentality then they will attract more of that.

Teach the child that they can't control how another person behaves towards them but they certainly can influence what they attract by virtue of what vibrational frequency they send out into the world. They must be able to hold this frequency for a reasonable period of time. Support them in holding the emotion and thought they desire to attract from others. If the child shows excessive fear or a state of constant weakness the school bully will pick up on that weakness and direct their bullying energy towards the child that is in that weak state. But if a child is confidently happy and playing with lots of friends in a powerful state of mind without fear the school bully is less likely to pick on an empowered confident child. You only attract what you are a vibrational match to.

Preparing children for Oneness of mankind.

It doesn't take a genius to see the direction the world is taking. Our resources are becoming limited, we are over populated and humanity in general is dangerously heading towards a third world war. With nuclear weapons at hand a world war would leave a tremendous trail of devastation if anything was left afterwards. If this happens these children will be the ones responsible for rebuilding a new society and new way of thinking.

We can teach them we live in a co-dependent universe where every human plays an essential role in society. Don't think for a moment that we don't all need each other! You can't through a stone in the ocean expecting to not create a ripple effect. Everything you do effects everyone around you. In essence you can't expect a human to take a life and not expect the effects to be felt on a wider scale. When this current way of thinking, educating and raising society eventually falls those left to pick up the pieces will need to have a different way of looking at the world to the current world we are in now.

There are now various intentional communities around the world using natural resources of the environment, swapping goods where they can and live as a supportive community taking turns to look after the children within the community they feel safe and supported by. In situations like this, the community must have a similar overview about life and open understanding and trust towards others.

This is the beginning of the movement towards an acceptance of the co-dependent world we live in. Rather than denying the co-dependence they are embracing it by working together towards common goals. The main goal being connection, equality and oneness of all mankind. If you watch Ants work together they are capable of creating amazing structures harmoniously, as a part of a community. Bees are the same. This is called the Hive mind. As humans we could call it the collective consciousness of our species. If you look up the 100th Monkey studies show how all species are connected by a Wi-Fi type of web/net and how they evolve as a species. Within a hive mind, each plays their very important role. Interesting how we are only figuring this out now yet we are supposed to be the most intelligent species living on earth.

Eric Pepin puts it beautifully in his books "I believe that the planet is a living organism floating in space. I believe that all the living creatures of the planet are part of the microorganisms to the Earth. I believe that the human race is the central nervous system of the planet." Eric Pepin – Higher Balance Institute. I recommend reading his book Handbook of the Navigator for those in search of meaning and a higher purpose to life.

Teach them to love themselves.

To save humanity as a whole we must first learn to nurture and love ourselves and once we are full of love we are then ready to give out. This is the natural spill over effect. If we have constantly enough food to eat we will never fear going hungry. Furthermore, if we have lots of food with always food to spare we are more likely to naturally and instinctually desire to share. Only a person who is in the constant state of fear of lacking something is likely to not to share or give anything away. The same goes for love. If a person fears that they lack love they will forever search for ways to get it from others thinking this will fill that void within them. Teal Swan's book Shadows Before Dawn is a great book that teaches about how to love yourself even after suffering the extraordinary circumstances that Teal suffered. Teal teaches people to ask themselves regularly, "What would someone who loves themselves do?" This question can be asked under any circumstances, when making a decision, from eating food to choosing what to wear and so on. Teach your children the same.

In the book the Celestine prophecy one of the insights mentioned in the book is the exchange of energy. It explains how each person has their own energy field. Children when being raised by society learn how to absorb or steal energy from others. Those with the ability to see auras can see this exchange of energy when people are talking to each other. As their energy fields connect there's usually one person whom might be sucking more energy from the other. Then after the interaction with that person the one who had their energy stolen feels tired and drained. There are many levels to this but I'm just mentioning a basic scenario.

In a Child's mind they think this is normal, that the only way to feel and become powerful is by absorbing energy from others. Not knowing that they can simply access this energy source themselves simply by having positive connections with people and the Earth and doing things that makes them feel joyful. They don't have to drain it or take it from others. There is enough energy power for everyone.

Teach children to respect their body

Don't force traditions onto children, if they don't wish to kiss or hug someone don't force them to do so. It's nice to see children naturally feel like going up to someone and giving them a comforting hug when they choose to. Making them do this is forcing them to be inauthentic. Maybe they don't feel the need or instinct to hug someone at moment in time. Watching them do it out of a pure desire to connect and show love to another human being is magical. This teaches them to honour their true feelings and instincts.

Being a Co-creator doesn't mean let kids be rude and get away with everything Remember that playing the gentle nurturing role of the Co-Creator does NOT mean that you allow your children to be rude or disrespectful towards you! You wouldn't be showing a good example of self-love if you allow anyone to treat you with disrespect or badly that includes your children. Don't allow your children to take advantage of you. There are times when children need to just get on with it and do what their parents have instructed them to do without arguments. Just like there are simple rules in society such as stopping at a red light, not stealing and more. Children need to understand that while they have the right to express themselves freely they still need to be able to follow rules that are in place if necessary for the harmony of all living in this world.

Being a Co-Creator most of the time

While it's ideal to be a Co-Creator example of a parent at best of the time give yourselves the permission to make occasional mistakes. The perfect parent doesn't exist and if a perfect parent did exist this parent would have to have some occasions where they make mistakes in order to use them as an example to their children of what good and bad parenting looks like.

Being able to make a mistake and correct it will offer the opportunity for a child to see the contrast between what good parenting looks like and what not so good parenting looks like. You can't have one without the other and both together will make a whole complete parenting experience. This is what we call the acceptance of the Shadow aspects of self. It will teach children to accept both aspects of their personality in order to understand and move towards what feels good for them. Maybe 20% of occasional bad parenting will make a child appreciate the 80% of mostly positive parenting. ☺

CHAPTER FOURTEEN

Becoming your authentic self

Doing Spray Tans as an extra income added so much more to my life than I thought it ever would. I thought it would be a simple mindless extra job, a means of extra income however that turned into a successful business. I provided not only a great Spray Tan but I was often called upon to offer some guidance and counselling to ladies in their most vulnerable state, without clothes on. I assure you this wasn't my intention it just happened. Girls would come in with all sorts of stories, my boyfriend is cheating, my husband got another Woman pregnant, my Son is a drug addict and so much more. I began to notice more and more that girls would come for a tan in a very timid, stressed or anxious state and were leaving confident, happy and calm. The reviews and feedback were so overwhelming. I even incorporated my intuitive abilities into my tanning sessions for those who also were interested at no extra charge.

I loved helping the clients look and feel amazing. I wanted them to come in one person and leave as a better more confident version of themselves, and I took pride in being a part of that.

Having Women take their clothes off in front of you makes you realize the complexities each one of them is dealing with. The self-talk was often, I'm too fat, I'm ugly, I stink, I'm too hairy, my toes are deformed, I'm too droopy …. You name it I heard it all! These poor Woman shouldn't have had to apologize or explain themselves to me. I was never one to have huge concerns around body image as I really didn't care what people thought of me by this point. Plus, I was raised around Portuguese and Brazilians who just love their food and the human body all shapes and sizes. My weight would fluctuate and I always looked curvy but I was always in full acceptance of what I looked like.

I had one lady come in once that just blew my mind. She was a larger lady but boy was her charisma larger. She said to me "I'm big and fat but I'm beautiful and I don't care what you think you still have to see and spray tan my big hairy Poonani!" She laughed! Her confidence and acceptance of self-radiated from her pores! Out of the thousands of clients I've tanned in my lifetime she was one that always stuck in my mind and it makes me smile every time I think of her.

If only Women could see themselves as I see them! They are all absolutely beautiful just as they are in their own way. My daughters used to comment on things I would wear but when they soon figured out I really didn't give a damn about what they thought of me they gave up commenting. One of my daughters called me Gloria from the kid's movie Madagascar. For those of you who don't know which character that is, She's the Hippopotamus. I'm a slightly chunkier lady but who cares if I don't. As long as there aren't any major health issues why should anyone have an opinion. I once asked my husband if he thinks

I'm fat? his answer was "You are very nutritious!" creative answer I thought and I couldn't argue with that Lol.

Today my clients know me as someone with little tolerance for bs. I have specific rules and expectations especially around business. I run it my way and if they respect me they will respect my rules if they want to do do business with me. This should be a daily mantra for all Women regardless of whether it's in business or relationships. If Women don't carry themselves with confidence on a daily basis and set their personal rules for how they expect people to interact with them they will forever be at the mercy of others.

A Woman should have enough confidence to be genuine with the world about who she is and what she expects of the world. Going about the world adhering to other people's needs or bowing down to others expectations will only create inauthentic resentful relationships.

I tell my clients to say how they honestly feel or what they expect from their relationship and they respond with complete fear of not being loved or fear of being abandoned! When in reality if their partner doesn't accept them for who they are or care about what makes them feel good then leaving would be doing them a huge favour actually! You can't put a gun to someone's head and say "Love me, please!" and expect an authentic love to be born out of that, and I sure as hell don't have to manipulate a Man into loving me Thank you very much!

We are at an age where everyone is constantly taking Selfies!! But where is the real self-love?? Woman portray themselves to be confident while taking selfies, yet put these girls in front of a mirror and tell them to say "I love you!! I accept you the way you are! I will always be there for you!" and guess what, they can't do it! Be genuine and authentic don't pretend to love yourself, LOVE YOURSELF!

Set your personal boundaries and demand that people respect them and you! They can't respect someone who is false to themselves, someone who doesn't know who they are internally or someone who isn't ok in their own company. Find ways to become happy within yourself, do things that bring you joy. After all, if you can't enjoy being with yourself, who else should have to tolerate you? You can lie to the world but you can't lie to yourself!

CHAPTER FIFTEEN
Men take the contraceptive Pill

I was incredibly interested to hear on the news the other day of the intention to bring in the Male Contraceptive Pill. The New Daily says "Australian researchers are developing a hormone-free male contraceptive pill that wouldn't impact libido or fertility, and believe it could be available in the next five to 10 years." It "would work by using chemicals that switch off two signalling proteins in the brain that causes sperm to be released" So the previous concerns around long-term irreversible fertility, birth defects and libido reduction from having used male hormones is no longer of concern. Thenewdaily.com.au

This was an animated conversation in my household. Does everyone realize what this could mean for the World?

Men haven't always had a huge amount of control over the pregnancy situation, either they wear a condom, use the withdrawal method or just simply don't have Sex so most of their options weren't the most pleasant. I wonder if Men will actually take more responsibility for prevention using this extra tool?

Men are usually the ones who would prefer to take their time considering very carefully whether they're ready to have children or not. I imagine Men having control over this and having the ability to prevent pregnancies would dramatically reduce the fluctuation in population. But that's just a personal opinion. There will be less unplanned pregnancies, a reduction in abortions and terminations, reduction in sterilisation operations and I believe that relationships would improve on so many levels.

In a relationship where both people have the power to prevent pregnancy there would have to be a need for greater communication skills in order for family planning to go ahead. There is no longer the ability for one to trick, manipulate or force the other into pregnancy, it will 'have to' be a mutual agreement now. People may actually begin to focus more on creating a happy, connected, stable and honest relationship over the need to simply procreate.

The roles being reversed may take Women some time to adapt to. In the past Women were able to say "whoops, I forgot to take the pill" now I wonder how Women will feel when a Man looks at them and says "Whoops, Sorry 'I' forgot to take the pill" Now it's the Woman's turn to completely freak out!

I imagine the opinion on this topic will be different in every part of the World. There will be the old fashioned who believe in leaving well enough alone and just letting nature take its course. There will be the anti-pharmaceuticals people saying that it's not natural and dangerous for health. There will be the religious people who may reject it. There will be the lower socio-economic people that will say they can't afford it. There will be the self-righteous Women who will down right condemn not having power over it. There will be some Men who will fear its implications around losing relationships or possible partnerships.

However, one of the concerns I might have would be over the increase in Sexually Transmitted Diseases. Having more freedom to do as Men wish without risk of consequences may encourage more promiscuous activity.

Interestingly when I started a discussion about this on Facebook not many people seemed to support the idea. And most people believed that Men would just simply forget and not take responsibility for taking the Pill. What are your thoughts around this topic?

CHAPTER SIXTEEN
Getting ready for kids

Self-acceptance

First and foremost, the most important thing to consider before having kids is love and acceptance for yourself as #1 priority. How much love and accept do you have for yourself, do you love and accept yourself unconditionally faults and all, Good and Bad? Are you so full of love within you that you are now ready to give out to another human being? Only when your cup is full that you are over flowing are you then ready to give out to someone else.

Likewise, only when you are so full of love and acceptance for who you are can you give that exact same thing to another human being. You can't give what you don't already have within yourself. Love is an infinite resource that never runs out. It simply grows and is shared. If you perceive that there is a lack of love within you then you will struggle to give what you think you may run out of. When you understand that loving yourself is simply the first step before loving someone else this is when you should consider having children or any other relationships for that matter.

Support

Make sure you have a good support system in place. Partner, parents, friends, family whoever you can call on if times get tough. Just knowing where to go in case of unexpected challenges such as breastfeeding support, depression or illness. Being able to seek help and the right supports the moment you feel a bad day or phase coming on will be your saviour in the long run. It doesn't make you a bad parent it makes you a more intelligent parent and one who considers your welfare and the welfare of your child as the utmost priority.

Research

Research and learn as much as you can around pregnancy, birth, breastfeeding, parenting and child development. This knowledge will be very valuable in the long run. Become clear on your ideas, expectations and beliefs around how you want your parenting experience to look like. No one is saying you can't change and fine tune along the way but it's good to understand yourself, your beliefs and foundations before you start. That way you have a point of reflection so you can see how far you have come and how much you have evolved.

Personal goals

If there's specific goals you'd like to achieve such as studies, travelling, career do it before you have children. Having children doesn't make these goals impossible but it makes them harder to achieve or it could take longer to achieve than expected. Avoid the possibility of resentments coming up towards your parenting responsibility and make sure your life is in order before having children.

Confidence around Children

Spend as much time around children as possible. Interestingly there's a few types of people, those who have more patience for other people's children and when they see other people's kids they always come up with the comment "Oh how cute" then when it comes to their own children they are less forgiving. These people after having children soon realise that maybe they weren't cut out for parenting.

There's also those who become more biased and over protective of their own children and criticise everyone else's children. Then there's those people who just absolutely love all children and have all the time in the world for them never thinking "Oh my gosh when can I hand this child back". These people accept all children for who and what they are, as little evolving people.

When you can look at all children and see through them only to feel what they are trying to express or be without judgement are you ready for the Co-creator role. Children aren't like broken toys you hand back to the store for replacement. They are for life, so make sure you are comfortable in the company of children constantly before considering having a child.

Look within

Do lots of Inner Child work! Learn to have compassion towards your own childhood concerns and your childhood experiences. Understanding your own upbringing and possible traumatic events that took place when you were a child will help you see into and feel your own child. If you are able to be present and non-judgmental towards your own inner child, you are more likely to be compassionate towards your own child.

Establish boundaries

Learn how to respect yourself enough to set good boundaries. Learn how to say "No!" If you are someone that doesn't like confrontation and would prefer to politely agree rather than stand up for yourself this is exactly what you will be demonstrating to your child. Unfortunately, it's these children who will attract bullying and other people who will abuse of their kindness. Begin to create strong virtuous gifts of character that define you as an individual

and that you would be proud enough to stand up for.
Teach your children how to stand up for themselves!

Plan your pregnancy

Plan for your pregnancy if planning is a possibility? Make sure all parties are in agreement with the decision to have a child. This helps to eliminate the tendency towards blame and an imbalance in parenting responsibilities. Spiritual teachers say that having a baby is an agreement between 3 souls, mum, dad and child.

The importance of breastfeeding

Consider breastfeeding as a high priority. Do all you can to get the support you need to ensure successfully breastfeeding your child. Breastfeeding is a gift only the mother can give. The connection between mother and child whilst breastfeeding has the power to heal and open the heart to higher dimensions. These days' birth is becoming such a violent process with so much intervention and leaving women powerless to their natural gift of birth. I encourage breastfeeding especially as a form of healing, connection and rebalancing after such a traumatic of birth. Breastfeeding has been known to substantially reduce the risk of postnatal depression as well as many other medical conditions post nataly for both mother and child.

and for those deciding to have more kids:

Look at your lifestyle

Knowing what the right age gap is for you. Look at your lifestyle, commitments and time available carefully. If you are wanting to spend quality time with each child having a reasonable gap so that one child is in childcare, school or occasionally babysat by a family member while you spend one on one time with the other can be a good option.
If you are a con dent parent who feels that you prefer to do the parenting all at once you may choose to have the children closer in age. Children generally with an age gap of 3 to 4 years still have a good connection without putting too much stress on you as a parent. In the case with multiple births obviously this isn't an option, but the main idea is to consider your limitations carefully and look at what's best for you, the child and the family as a whole before considering more kids.

Know your limits

Sometimes we get quiet, easy children who don't challenge us too much. Then we have more children under the false belief that they will all be the same only to get a spirited child. Make sure you understand your own limits. If you are already feeling under pressure or are prone to anxiety with the child/children, you already have use common sense and consider carefully whether it's a good idea to have any more children right now. Don't continue to have children if you feel as though you aren't coping. Consider whether in fact you are having children for your own personal desires or because you are con dent in your parenting role and have a lot time and attention to give to an extra child. The difference is basing the focus of this decision on what you can get out of an extra child or what you can offer to an extra child. Are you making it about you or the new child?

Does gender matter?

Waiting for the desired gender. It's common for people who've had numerous of only one gender to consider trying again for the opposite sex. The reality is you could very well get another of the same sex. Are you open and ready for this possibility? How comfortable are you with the idea of just having all children of one gender?

You come first

Continue to look after yourself!! Love yourself!! Take the time to continue to do things that give you joy and feel like your old self again. It can be easy to lose yourself in your daily chores taking care of the children. Connect with yourself daily as it's easy to lose yourself in the role of parenting the more children you have. Mirror work taught by Louise L. Hay is a great idea. Making sure you are feeling good will teach your child to also value and take care of themselves.

Recognising the finish line

Knowing when you are done! Internally you can feel when you're ready to close that chapter of your life and move onto the next phase in life.

It's important to weigh up the pros and cons of having more children or stopping where you are. Making an informed and well thought out decision will ensure that your decision won't be one you look back on with regret. Accepting this new phase can feel a little sad but when you are absolutely ready it can be a joyful and liberating one. Allow yourself the time to go through the stages of grief if necessary. The relief of the next phase is that the next children to come into your family will be your grandchildren and grandchildren can always be handed back to their parents. Therefore, you can enjoy them but have minimal responsibility over them. Co-creating as a grandparent is one of choice, not of obligation.

Just on a side note:

If you are someone who is questioning whether you should be having children or not, and taking your time to seriously consider whether you are ready or not, then you are one of the rare quality people who cares about this decision and probably 'should' be having children! It's those people who are careless about having child after child without any consideration that should be more mindful.

CHAPTER SEVENTEEN
P.S.

I hope that my parenting journey will inspire everyone towards a rewarding parenting experience of their own. Becoming a parent is an awakening experience. Giving birth itself and going through all that pain where you literally think you are going to die is almost like a rite of passage, an initiation process per se to maturity.

I extended my studies to becoming a Doula (Birthing Assistant) and Breastfeeding Counsellor. That's how passionate I am about this process and how much I just absolutely love being a Mum today. Watching parents thrive and make the most of the joyous experience that is parenting gives me so much joy. Appreciating it for the growth promoting experience that it can be.

Parenting has made me grow in ways I never imagined possible. I wish this growth upon everyone that is wanting to evolve. Being a parent will make you understand what real love and compassion is. It will open up your heart centre and make you look at life differently. Having children teaches your heart to Love to a capacity you never imagined possible. Having children creates an awareness and understanding of the fragility and sensitivity of the precious gift that is life!

However, we mustn't forget that our children are growing alongside us, with us. Whatever decisions we make will affect them also. So, think carefully before you choose to parent another human being. Keep evolving while helping that little Human evolve too.

Thank you!

www.ingramcontent.com/pod-product-compliance
Lightning Source LLC
Chambersburg PA
CBHW070256010526
44107CB00056B/2481